The Mou Bride

By
William Congreve

ANODOS
BOOKS

William Congreve (1670-1729)
Originally published in 1703.

Anodos Books
1c Kings Road
Whithorn
Newton Stewart
Dumfries & Galloway
DG8 8PP

Contents

Prologue   1

Preface   3

Dramatis Personæ   5

Act I.   7

    Scene I.   7

Act II.   19

    Scene I.   19

    Scene II.   21

Act III.   31

    Scene I.   31

Act IV.   43

    Scene I.   43

Act V.   55

    Scene I.   55

    Scene II.   58

Epilogue   67

Prologue

THE Time has been when Plays were not so plenty,
And a less Number New would well content ye.
New Plays did then like Almanacks appear;
And One was thought sufficient for a Year:
Tho' they are more like Almanacks of late;
For in one Year, I think, they're out of Date.
Nor were they without Reason join'd together;
For just as one prognosticates the Weather,
How plentiful the Crop, or scarce the Grain,
What Peals of Thunder, and what Show'rs of Rain;
So t'other can foretel, by certain Rules,
What Crops of Coxcombs, or what Floods of Fools.
In such like Prophecies were Poets skill'd,
Which now they find in their own Tribe fulfill'd:
The Dearth of Wit they did so long presage,
Is fall'n on us, and almost starves the Stage.
Were you not griev'd, as often as you saw
Poor Actors thresh such empty Sheafs of Straw?
Toiling and lab'ring, at their Lungs Expence,
To start a Jest, or force a little Sence.
Hard Fate for us! still harder in th' Event;
Our Authors Sin, but we alone Repent.
Still they proceed, and, at our Charge, write worse;
'Twere some Amends if they could reimburse:
But there's the Devil, tho' their Cause is lost,
There's no recovering Damages or Cost.
Good Wits, forgive this Liberty we take,
Since Custom gives the Losers leave to speak.
But if provok'd, your dreadful Wrath remains,
Take your Revenge upon the coming Scenes:
For that damn'd Poet's spar'd who Damns a Brother,
As one Thief 'scapes, that Executes another.
Thus far alone does to the Wits relate;
But from the rest we hope a better Fate.
To please and move has been our Poet's Theme,
Art may direct, but Nature is his aim;
And Nature miss'd, in vain he boasts his Art,
For only Nature can affect the Heart.
Then freely judge the Scenes that shall ensue,
But as with Freedom, judge with Candour too.
He wou'd not lose thro Prejudice his Cause;
Nor wou'd obtain precariously Applause.
Impartial Censure he requests from all,
Prepar'd, by just Decrees to stand, or fall.

Preface

THAT high Station, which by Your Birth You hold above the People, exacts from every one, as a Duty, whatever Honours they are capable of paying to Your Royal Highness: But that more exalted Place, to which Your Vertues have rais'd You, above the rest of Princes, makes the Tribute of our Admiration and Praise, rather a Choice more immediately preventing that Duty.

The Publick Gratitude is ever founded on a Publick Benefit; and what is universally bless'd, is always an universal Blessing. Thus from Your self we derive the Offerings which we bring; and the Incense which arises to Your Name, only returns to its Original, and but naturally requires the Parent of its Being.

From hence it is that this Poem, constituted on a Moral, whose End is to recommend and to encourage Vertue, of consequence has recourse to Your Royal Highness's Patronage; aspiring to cast it self beneath Your Feet, and declining Approbation, till You shall condescend to own it, and vouchsafe to shine upon it as on a Creature of Your Influence.

'Tis from the Example of Princes that Vertue becomes a Fashion in the People, for even they who are averse to Instruction, will yet be fond of Imitation.

But there are Multitudes, who never can have Means nor Opportunities of so near an Access, as to partake of the Benefit of such Examples. And to these, Tragedy, which distinguishes it self from the Vulgar Poetry by the Dignity of its Characters, may be of Use and Information. For they who are at that distance from Original Greatness, as to be depriv'd of the Happiness of Contemplating the Perfections and real Excellencies of Your Royal Highness's Person in Your Court, may yet behold some small Sketches and Imagings of the Vertues of Your Mind, abstracted, and represented in the Theatre.

Thus Poets are instructed, and instruct; not alone by Precepts which persuade, but also by Examples which illustrate. Thus is Delight interwoven with Instruction; when not only Vertue is prescrib'd, but also represented.

But if we are delighted with the Liveliness of a feign'd Representation of Great and Good Persons and their Actions, how must we be charm'd with beholding the Persons themselves? If one or two excelling Qualities, barely touch'd in the single Action and small Compass of a Play, can warm an Audience, with a Concern and Regard even for the seeming Success and Prosperity of the Actor: With what Zeal must the Hearts of all be fill'd, for the continued and encreasing Happiness of those, who are the true and living Instances of Elevated and Persisting Vertue? Even the Vicious themselves must have a secret Veneration for those peculiar Graces and Endowments, which are daily so eminently conspicuous in Your Royal Highness; and though repining, feel a Pleasure which in spite of Envy they per-force approve.

If in this piece, humbly offer'd to Your Royal Highness, there shall appear the

Resemblance of any one of those many Excellencies which You so promiscuously possess, to be drawn so as to merit Your least Approbation, it has the End and Accomplishment of its Design. And however imperfect it may be in the Whole, through the Inexperience or Incapacity of the Author, yet, if there is so much as to convince Your Royal Highness, that a Play may be with Industry so dispos'd (in spight of the licentious Practice of the Modern Theatre) as to become sometimes an innocent, and not unprofitable Entertainment; it will abundantly gratifie the Ambition, and Recompence the Endeavours of,

Your Royal Highness's
Most Obedient, and
most humbly Devoted Servant,
WILLIAM CONGREVE. (1697).

Dramatis Personæ

Men

MANUEL, *the King of* Granada.

GONSALEZ, *his favourite.*

GARCIA, *son to* Gonsalez.

PEREZ, *Captain of the* Guards.

ALONZO, *an officer, creature to* Gonsalez.

OSMYN, *a noble prisoner.*

HELI, *a prisoner, his friend.*

SELIM, *an* Eunuch

Women

ALMERIA, *the Princess of* Granada.

ZARA, *a captive* Queen.

LEONORA, *chief attendant on the* Princess.

Women, Eunuchs, and Mutes attending Zara. *Guards, etc...*

SCENE Granada.

Act I.

Scene I.

A Room of State.

The Curtain rising slowly to soft Musick, discovers Almeria *in Mourning,* Leonora *waiting in Mourning.*

After the Musick Almeria *rises from her Chair, and comes forward.*

Alm. Musick has Charms to sooth a savage Breast,
To soften Rocks, or bend a knotted Oak.
I've read, that things inanimate have mov'd,
And, as with living Souls, have been inform'd,
By Magick Numbers and persuasive Sound.
What then am I? Am I more senseless grown
Than Trees, or Flint? O force of constant Woe!
'Tis not in Harmony to calm my Griefs.
Anselmo sleeps, and is at Peace; last Night
The silent Tomb receiv'd the good old King;
He and his Sorrows now are safely lodg'd
Within its cold, but hospitable Bosom.
Why am not I at Peace?

Leon. For Heaven's sake, dear Madam, moderate
Your Griefs, there is no Cause—

Alm. Peace—No Cause! yes, there is Eternal Cause,
And Misery Eternal will succeed.
Thou canst not tell—thou hast indeed no Cause.

Leo. Believe me, Madam, I lament *Anselmo*,
And always did compassionate his Fortune;
Have often wept, to see how cruelly
Your Father kept in Chains his Fellow-King:
And oft at Night, when all have been retir'd,
Have stoln from Bed, and to his Prison crept;
Where, while his Gaoler slept, I thro' the Grate
Have softly whisper'd, and enquir'd his Health;
Sent in my Sighs and Pray'rs for his Deliv'rance;
For Sighs and Pray'rs were all that I could offer.

Alm. Indeed thou hast a soft and gentle Nature,
That thus couldst melt to see a Stranger's Wrongs.
O *Leonora*, hadst thou known *Anselmo*,
How would thy Heart have bled to see his Suff'rings.
Thou hadst no Cause, but general Compassion.

Leo. My Love of you, my Royal Mistress, gave me Cause,
My Love of you begot my Grief for him;
For I had heard, that when the Chance of War
Had bless'd *Anselmo*'s Arms with Victory,

7

And the rich Spoil of all the Field, and you,
The Glory of the whole, were made the Prey
Of his Success; that then, in spite of Hate,
Revenge, and that Hereditary Feud
Entail'd between *Valentia's* and *Granada's* Kings,
He did endear himself to your Affection,
By all the worthy and indulgent Ways
His most industrious Goodness cou'd invent;
Proposing by a Match between *Alphonso*
His Son, the brave *Valentia* Prince, and you,
To end the long Dissention, and unite
The jarring Crowns.

Alm. O *Alphonso! Alphonso!* thou art too
At Peace; Father and Son are now no more—
Then why am I? O when shall I have Rest?
Why do I live to say you are no more?
Why are all these things thus?—
Is there necessity I must be miserable?
Is it of moment to the Peace of Heav'n
That I should be afflicted thus?—If not,
Why is it thus contriv'd? Why are all things laid
By some unseen Hand, so, as of consequence
They must to me bring Curses, Grief of Heart,
The last Distress of Life, and sure Despair.

Leo. Alas, you search too far, and think too deeply

Alm. Why was I carried to *Anselmo's* Court?
Or, when there, why was I us'd so tenderly?
Why did he not use me like an Enemy?
For so my Father would have us'd his Child.
O *Alphonso, Alphonso!*
Devouring Seas have wash'd thee from my sight,
But there's no time shall rase thee from my Memory
No, I will live to be thy Monument;
The cruel Ocean would deprive thee of a Tomb,
But in my Heart thou art interr'd; there, there,
Thy dear Resemblance is for ever fix'd;
My Love, my Lord, my Husband still, though lost.

Leo. Husband! O Heav'ns!

Alm. What have I said?
My Grief has hurry'd me beyond all Thought.
I would have kept that secret; though I know
Thy Love and Faith to me deserve all Confidence.
But 'tis the Wretches Comfort still to have
Some small Reserve of near and inward Woe,
Some unsuspected Hoard of darling Grief,
Which they unseen may wail, and weep, and mourn,

8

And Glutton-like alone devour.

Leo. Indeed I knew not this.

Alm. O no, thou know'st not half—thou know'st nothing—
—If thou didst!—
If I should tell thee, wouldst thou pity me?
Tell me: I know thou wou'dst, thou art compassionate.

Leo. Witness these Tears.—

Alm. I thank thee—indeed I do—
I thank thee, that thou'lt pity thy sad Mistress;
For 'tis the poor Prerogative of Greatness,
To be wretched and unpitied—
But I did promise I would tell thee—What?
My Griefs? Thou do'st already know 'em:
And when I said thou didst know nothing,
It was because thou didst not know *Alphonso:*
For to have known my Loss, thou must have known
His Worth, his Truth, and tenderness of Love.

Leo. The Memory of that brave Prince stands fair
In all Report—
And I have heard imperfectly his Loss;
But fearful to renew your Troubles past,
I never did presume to ask the Story.

Alm. If for my swelling Heart I can, I'll tell thee.
I was a welcome Captive in *Valentia,*
Ev'n on the Day when *Manuel,* my Father,
Led on his conqu'ring Troops, high as the Gates
Of King *Anselmo's* Palace; which in Rage,
And Heat of War, and dire Revenge, he fir'd.
Whilst the good King, to shun approaching Flames,
Started amidst his Foes, and made Captivity his Refuge.
Would I had perish'd in those Flames—
But 'twas not so decreed.
Alphonso, who foresaw my Father's Cruelty,
Had born the Queen and me on board a Ship
Ready to sail, and when this News was brought
We put to Sea; but being betray'd by some
Who knew our Flight, we closely were pursu'd,
And almost taken; when a sudden Storm
Drove us, and those that follow'd, on the Coast
Of *Africk:* There our Vessel struck the Shoar,
And bulging 'gainst a Rock was dash'd in pieces.
But Heaven spared me for yet more Affliction!
Conducting them who follow'd us to shun
The Shoal, and save me floating on the Waves,
While the good Queen and my *Alphonso* perish'd.

9

Leo. Alas! were you then wedded to *Alphonso?*

Alm. That Day, that fatal Day, our Hands were join'd;
For when my Lord beheld the Ship pursuing,
And saw her Rate so far exceeding ours;
He came to me, and begg'd me by my Love,
I would consent the Priest might make us one;
That whether Death, or Victory ensu'd,
I might be his, beyond the Power of future Fate:
The Queen too did assist his Suit—I granted,
And in one Day, was wedded, and a Widow.

Leo. Indeed 'twas mournful—

Alm. 'Twas that,
For which I mourn, and will for ever mourn;
Nor will I change these black and dismal Robes,
Or ever dry these swol'n and watry Eyes;
Or ever taste Content, or Peace of Heart,
While I have Life, or Memory of my *Alphonso.*

Leo. Look down, good Heav'n, with Pity on her Sorrows,
And grant, that Time may bring her some Relief.

Alm. O no! Time gives Encrease to my Afflictions.
The circling Hours, that gather all the Woes,
Which are diffus'd thro' the revolving Year,
Come, heavy-laden with the oppressing Weight,
To me; with me, successively, they leave
The Sighs, the Tears, the Groans, the restless Cares,
And all the Damps of Grief, that did retard their Flight;
They shake their downy Wings, and scatter all
The dire collected Dews on my poor Head;
Then flie with Joy and Swiftness from me.

Leo. Hark!
The distant Shouts proclaim your Father's Triumph;

[*Shouts at a distance.*

O cease, for Heaven's sake, asswage a little
This Torrent of your Grief; for, much I fear
It will incense him, thus to see you drown'd
In Tears, when Joy appears in ev'ry other Face.

Alm. And Joy he brings to ev'ry other Heart,
But double, double weight of Woe to mine;
For with Him *Garcia* comes—*Garcia,* to whom
I must be sacrific'd, and all the Faith
And Vows I gave my dear *Alphonso,* basely
Violated—
No, it shall never be; for I will die first,
Die Ten thousand Deaths—Look down, look down,

10

[*Kneels.*

Alphonso, hear the Sacred Vow I make;
Leave for a Moment to behold Eternal Bliss,
And bend thy glorious Eyes to Earth and me;
And thou *Anselmo,* if yet thou art arriv'd
Thro' all Impediments of purging Fire,
To that bright Heav'n, where my *Alphonso* reigns,
Behold thou also, and attend my Vow.
If ever I do yield, or give Consent,
By any Action, Word or Thought, to Wed
Another Lord; may then just Heav'n show'r down
Unheard of Curses on me, greater far
(If such there be in angry Heav'n's Vengeance)
Than any I have yet endur'd.—And now

[*Rising.*

Methinks my Heart has some Relief: Having
Discharg'd this Debt, incumbent on my Love.
Yet, one thing more I would engage from thee.

Leo. My Heart, my Life and Will, are only yours.

Alm. I thank thee. 'Tis but this; anon, when all
Are busied in the general Joy, that thou
Wilt privately with me
Steal forth, and visit good *Anselmo*'s Tomb.

Leo. Alas! I fear some fatal Resolution.

Alm. No, on my Life, my Faith, I mean no Violence.
I feel I'm more at large,
Since I have made this Vow:
Perhaps I would repeat it there more solemnly.
'Tis that, or some such melancholy Thought,
Upon my Word no more.

Leo. I will attend you.

Enter *Alonzo.*

Alon. The Lord *Gonsalez* comes to tell your Highness
Of the King's approach.

Alm. Conduct him in.

[Exit *Alon.*

That's his Pretence, I know his Errand is
To fill my Ears with *Garcia*'s valiant Deeds;
And with his artful Tongue, to gild and magnifie
His Son's Exploits.
But I am arm'd with Ice around my Heart,
Not to be warm'd with Words, nor idle Eloquence.

Enter *Gonsalez.*

11

[Bowing very humbly.

Gons. Be ev'ry Day of your long Life like this.
The Sun, bright Conquest, and your brighter Eyes,
Have all conspir'd to blaze promiscuous Light,
And bless this Day with most unequal Lustre.
Your Royal Father, my Victorious Lord,
Loaden with Spoils, and ever-living Laurel,
Is entring now in Martial Pomp the Palace.
Five hundred Mules precede his solemn March,
Which groan beneath the Weight of *Moorish* Wealth.
Chariots of War, adorn'd with glittering Gems,
Succeed; and next, a hundred neighing Steeds,
White as the fleecy Rain on *Alpine* Hills;
That bound, and foam, and champ the Golden Bit,
As they disdain'd the Victory they grace.
Prisoners of War in shining Fetters follow;
And Captains of the Noblest Blood of *Africk*
Sweat by his Chariot Wheel, and lick and grind,
With gnashing Teeth, the Dust his Triumphs raise.
The swarming Populace spread every Wall,
And cling, as if with Claws they did enforce
Their Hold, thro' clifted Stones, stretching and staring,
As if they were all of Eyes, and every Limb
Would feed his Faculty of Admiration.
While you alone retire, and shun this Sight;
This Sight, which is indeed not seen (tho' twice
The Multitude should gaze)
In Absence of your Eyes.

Alm. My Lord, my Eyes ungratefully behold
The gilded Trophies of exterior Honours.
Nor will my Ears be charm'd with sounding Words,
Or pompous Phrase; the Pageantry of Souls.
But that my Father is return'd in Safety,
I bend to Heav'n with Thanks and humble Praise.

Gons. Excellent Princess!
But 'tis a Task unfit for my weak Age,
With dying Words, to offer at your Praise.
Garcia, my Son, your Beauty's lowest Slave,
Has better done;
In proving with his Sword, upon your Foes,
The Force and Influence of your matchless Charms.

Alm. I doubt not of the worth of *Garcia's* Deeds,
Which had been brave, tho' I had ne'er been born.

Leo. Madam, the King.

[Flourish.

12

Alm. My Women. I wou'd meet him.

[Attendants to *Almeria* enter in Mourning.

Symphony of Warlike Musick. Enter the *King,* attended by *Garcia* and several
Officers. Files of Prisoners in Chains, and Guards, who are ranged in Order
round the Stage. *Almeria* meets the King, and kneels; afterwards *Gonsalez*
kneels and kisses the King's Hand, while *Garcia* does the same to the Princess.

King. Almeria, rise—My best *Gonsalez* rise.
What, Tears! my good old Friend.—

Gons. But Tears of Joy. To see you thus, has fill'd
My Eyes with more Delight than they can hold.

King. By Heav'n thou lov'st me, and I'm pleas'd thou dost:
Take it for Thanks, Old Man, that I rejoice
To see thee weep on this Occasion—But some
Here are who seem to mourn at our Success!
How is it, *Almeria,* that you meet our Eyes,
Upon this solemn Day, in these sad Weeds?
You and yours, are all, in opposition
To my Brightness, like Daughters of Affliction.

Alm. Forgive me, Sir, if I offend.
The Year, which I have vow'd to pay to Heav'n,
In Mourning and strict Life, for my Deliverance
From Death, and Wreck of the tempestuous-Sea,
Wants yet to be expired.

King. Your Zeal to Heav'n is great; so is your Debt:
Yet something too is due to me, who gave
That Life, which Heav'n preserv'd. A Day bestow'd
In Filial Duty, had atton'd and giv'n
A Dispensation to your Vow—No more.
'Twas weak and wilful—and a Woman's Error.
Yet—upon thought, it doubly wounds my Sight,
To see that Sable worn upon the Day
Succeeding that, in which our deadliest Foe,
Hated *Anselmo,* was interr'd—By Heav'n,
It looks as thou didst mourn for him: Just as
Thy senseless Vow appear'd to bear its Date,
Not from that Hour wherein thou wert preserv'd,
But that wherein the curs'd *Alphonso* perish'd.
Ha! what? thou dost not weep to think of that?

Gons. Have Patience, Royal Sir, the Princess weeps
To have offended you. If Fate decreed,
One pointed Hour should be *Alphonso*'s Loss,
And her Deliverance; is she to blame?

King. I tell thee she's to blame, not to have feasted
When my first Foe was laid in Earth, such Enmity,

13

Such Detestation, bears my Blood to his;
My Daughter should have revell'd at his Death.
She should have made these Palace Walls to shake,
And all this high and ample Roof to ring
With her Rejoicings. What, to mourn, and weep;
Then, then to weep, and pray, and grieve? By Heav'n,
There's not a Slave, a shackled Slave of mine,
But should have smil'd that Hour, through all his Care,
And shook his Chains in Transport and rude Harmony.

Gons. What she has done, was in excess of Goodness;
Betray'd by too much Piety, to seem
As if she had offended.

King. To seem is to commit, at this Conjuncture.
I wonnot have the seeming of a Sorrow seen
To Day—Retire, divest your self with speed
Of that offensive Black; on me be all
The Violation of your Vow.
You stand excused that I command it.

Gar. (*kneeling.*) Your Pardon, Sir, if I presume so far,
As to remind you of your gracious Promise.

King. Rise, *Garcia*—I forgot. Yet stay, *Almeria.*

Alm. O my boding Heart—What is your Pleasure, Sir?

King. Draw near, and give your Hand; and, *Garcia,* yours:
Receive this Lord, as one whom I have found
Worthy to be your Husband, and my Son.

Gar. Thus let me kneel to take—O not to take,
But to devote, and yield my self for ever
The Slave and Creature of my Royal Mistress.

Gons. O let me prostrate pay my worthless Thanks
For this high Honour.

King. No more; my Promise long since pass'd, thy Loyalty,
And *Garcia's* well-try'd Valour, all oblige me.
This Day we Triumph; but to Morrow's Sun
Shall shine on *Garcia's* Nuptials.

Alm. Oh!—

[*Faints.*

Gar. Alas, she faints! help to support her.

Gons. She recovers.

King. A Bridal Qualm; soon off. How is't, *Almeria?*

Alm. A sudden Chilness seizes on my Spirits.
Your Leave, Sir, to retire.

King. Garcia, Conduct her.

Garcia leads *Almeria* to the Door, and returns.

This idle Vow hangs on her Woman's Fears.
I'll have a Priest shall Preach her from her Faith,
And make it Sin, not to renounce that Vow
Which I'd have broken.

[*Trumpets.*

Enter Alonzo.

Offic. The beauteous Captive, *Zara*, is arriv'd,
And with a Train as if she still were Wife
To *Albucacim,* and the *Moor* had conquer'd.

King. It is our Will she should be so attended.
Bear hence these Prisoners. *Garcia,* which is he,
Of whose mute Valour you relate such Wonders?

[*Prisoners led off.*

Gar. Osmyn, who led the *Moorish* Horse; he does;
Great Sir, at her Request, attend on *Zara.*

King. He is your Prisoner, as you please dispose him.

Gar. I would oblige him, but he shuns my Kindness;
And with a haughty Mien, and stern Civility,
Humbly declines all Offers: If he speak
'Tis scarce above a Word; as he were born
Alone to do, and did disdain to talk;
At least, to talk where he must not command.

King. Such Sullenness, and in a Man so brave,
Must have some other Cause than his Captivity.
Did *Zara,* then, request he might attend her?

Gar. My Lord, she did.

King. That, join'd with his Behaviour,
Begets a Doubt. I'd have 'em watch'd; perhaps
Her Chains hang heavier on him than his own.

Flourish; and Enter *Zara* and *Osmyn* bound; conducted by *Perez* and a Guard,
and attended by *Selim* and several Mutes and Eunuchs in a Train.

King. What Welcome, and what Honours, beauteous *Zara,*
A King and Conqueror can give, are yours.
A Conqueror indeed, where you are won;
Who with such Lustre strike admiring Eyes,
That had our Pomp been with your Presence grac'd,
Th' expecting Crowd had been deceiv'd; and seen
Their Monarch enter not Triumphant, but
In Triumph led; your Beauty's Slave.

Zara. If I on any Terms could condescend
To like Captivity, or think those Honours,

15

Which Conquerors in Courtesie bestow,
Of equal Value with unborrow'd Rule,
And Native Right to Arbitrary Sway;
I might be pleas'd, when I behold this Train
With usual Homage wait. But when I feel
These Bonds, I look with Loathing on my self;
And scorn vile Slavery, tho' doubly hid
Beneath Mock-Praises, and dissembled State.

King. Those Bonds! 'Twas my Command you should be free.
How durst you, *Perez,* disobey me?

Perez. Great Sir,
Your Order was, she should not wait your Triumph;
But at some distance follow, thus attended.

King. 'Tis false; 'twas more; I bad she should be free:
If not in Words, I bad it by my Eyes.
Her Eyes did more than bid—Free her and hers
With speed—yet stay—my Hands alone can make
Fit Restitution here—Thus I release you,
And by releasing you enslave my self.

Zara. Favours conferr'd, tho' when unsought, deserve
Acknowledgment from Noble Minds. Such Thanks
As one hating to be oblig'd—
Yet hating more Ingratitude, can pay,
I offer.

King. Born to Excel, and to Command!
As by transcendent Beauty to attract
All Eyes, so by Preheminence of Soul
To rule all Hearts.
Garcia, what's he, who with contracted Brow,

[Beholding *Osmyn* as they unbind him.

And sullen Port, glooms downward with his Eyes;
At once regardless of his Chains, or Liberty?

Gar. That, Sir, is *Osmyn.*

King. He answers well the Character you gave him.
Whence comes it, Valiant *Osmyn,* that a Man
So great in Arms, as thou art said to be,
So ill can brook Captivity,
The common Chance of War?

Osm. Because Captivity has robb'd me of a just Revenge.

King. I understand not that.

Osm. I would not have you.

Zara. That Gallant *Moor* in Battel lost a Friend,
Whom more than Life he lov'd; and the Regret,

16

Of not revenging on his Foes that Loss,
Has caus'd this Melancholy and Despair.

King. She does excuse him; 'tis as I suspected.

[To *Gons.*

Gons. That Friend may be her self; show no Resentment
Of his Arrogance yet; she looks concern'd.

King. I'll have Enquiry made; his Friend may be
A Prisoner. His Name?

Zara.

Heli.

King. Garcia, be it your Care to make that search.
It shall be mine to pay Devotion here;
At this Fair Shrine to lay my Laurels down,
And raise Love's Altar on the Spoils of War.
Conquest and Triumph, now, are mine no more;
Nor will I Victory in Camps adore:
For, ling'ring there, in long suspence she stands,
Shifting the Prize in unresolving Hands:
Unus'd to wait, I broke through her Delay,
Fix'd her by Force, and snatch'd the doubtful Day.
But late I find that War is but her Sport;
In Love the Goddess keeps her awful Court:
Fickle in Fields, unsteadily she flies,
But Rules with settled Sway in *Zara*'s Eyes.

[Ex. Omnes.

17

Act II.

Scene I.

Representing the Isle of a Temple.

Enter *Garcia, Heli* and *Perez.*

Gar. THIS Way, we're told, *Osmyn* was seen to walk;
Chusing this lonely Mansion of the Dead,
To mourn, brave *Heli,* thy mistaken Fate.

Hel. Let Heav'n with Thunder to the Centre strike me,
If to arise in very Deed from Death,
And to revisit with my long clos'd Eyes
This living Light, could to my Soul, or Sense,
Afford a Thought, or Glimpse of Joy,
In least Proportion to the vast Delight
I feel, to hear of *Osmyn*'s Name; to hear
That *Osmyn* lives, and I again shall see him.

Gar. Unparallell'd Fidelity!
I've heard, with Admiration, of your Friendship;
And could, with equal Joy and Envy, view
The Transports of your Meeting.

Perez. Yonder, my Lord, behold the Noble *Moor.*

Hel. Where? where?

Gar. I see him not.

Perez. I saw him when I spoke, thwarting my View,
And striding with distemper'd Haste; his Eyes
Seem'd Flame, and flash'd upon me with a Glance;
Then forward shot their Fires, which he pursu'd,
As to some Object frightful, yet not fear'd.

Gar. Let's haste to follow him, and know the Cause.

Hel. My Lord, let me entreat you to forbear:
Leave me alone, to find and cure the Cause.
I know his Melancholy, and such Starts
Are usual to his Temper. It might raise him
To act some Violence upon himself,
So to be caught in an unguarded Hour,
And when his Soul gives all her Passions way,
Secure and loose in friendly Solitude.
I know his Noble Heart would burst with Shame,
To be surpriz'd by Strangers in its Frailty.

Gar. Go, gen'rous *Heli,* and relieve your Friend.
Far be it from me, officiously to pry
Or press upon the Privacies of others.

Hel. Y'are truly Noble.

19

Gar. Perez, the King expects from our Return
To have his Jealousie confirm'd, or clear'd,
Of that appearing Love which *Zara* bears
To *Osmyn;* but some other Opportunity
Must make that plain.

Perez. To me 'twas long since plain,
And ev'ry Look of his and hers confess it.

Gar. If so, Unhappiness attends their Love,
And I cou'd pity 'em. I hear some coming,
The Friends perhaps are met; let us avoid 'em.

[Exeunt.

Enter *Almeria* and *Leonora.*

Alm. It was a fancy'd Noise; for all is hush'd.

Leo. It bore the Accent of a Human Voice.

Alm. It was thy Fear, or else some transient Wind
Whistling thro' Hollows of the vaulted Isle.
We'll listen—

Leo. Hark!

Alm. No, all is hush'd, and still as Death—'Tis dreadful!
How rev'rend is the Face of this tall Pile,
Whose ancient Pillars rear their Marble Heads,
To bear aloft its arch'd and pond'rous Roof,
By its own Weight made stedfast and immoveable,
Looking Tranquility. It strikes an Awe
And Terror on my aking Sight; the Tombs
And Monumental Caves of Death look Cold,
And shoot a Chilness to my trembling Heart.
Give me thy Hand, and speak to me; nay, speak,
And let me hear thy Voice;
My own affrights me with its Eccho's.

Leo. Let us return; the Horror of this Place
And Silence, will encrease your Melancholy.

Alm. It may my Fears, but cannot add to that.
No, I will on; shew me *Anselmo's* Tomb,
Lead me o'er Bones and Skulls and mould'ring Earth
Of Human Bodies; for I'll mix with them,
Or wind me in the Shroud of some pale Coarse
Yet green in Earth, rather than be the Bride
Of *Garcia's* more detested Bed. That Thought
Exerts my Spirits; and my present Fears
Are lost in dread of greater Ill. Shew me,
Lead me, for I am bolder grown: Lead me

20

Where I may kneel and pay my Vows again
To him, to Heav'n, and my *Alphonso*'s Soul.

Leo. I go; but Heav'n can tell with what Regret.

[Exeunt.

Scene II.

The Scene opening discovers a Place of Tombs. One Monument fronting the
View greater than the rest.

Enter *Heli*.

Heli. I wander thro' this Maze of Monuments,
Yet cannot find him—Hark! sure 'tis the Voice
Of one complaining—There it sounds—I'll follow it.

[Exit.

Re-enter *Almeria* and *Leonora*.

Leo. Behold the Sacred Vault, within whose Womb
The poor Remains of good *Anselmo* rest;
Yet fresh and unconsum'd by Time or Worms.
What do I see? O Heav'n! either my Eyes
Are false, or still the Marble Door remains
Unclos'd; the Iron Grates that lead to Death
Beneath, are still wide stretch'd upon their Hinge,
And staring on us with unfolded Leaves.

Alm. Sure 'tis the friendly Yawn of Death for me;
And that dumb Mouth, significant in Show,
Invites me to the Bed where I alone
Shall rest; shews me the Grave, where Nature weary'd,
And long oppres'd with Woes and bending Cares,
May lay the Burden down, and sink in Slumbers
Of Eternal Peace. Death, grim Death, will fold
Me in his leaden Arms, and press me close
To his cold clayie Breast: My Father then
Will cease his Tyranny; and *Garcia* too
Will fly my pale Deformity with loathing.
My Soul, enlarg'd from its vile Bonds, will mount,
And range the Starry Orbs, and Milky Ways,
Of that refulgent World, where I shall swim
In liquid Light, and float on Seas of Bliss
To my *Alphonso*'s Soul. O Joy too great!
O Extasie of Thought! Help me, *Anselmo*;
Help me, *Alphonso*; take me, reach thy Hand;
To thee, to thee I call, to thee, *Alphonso*:
O *Alphonso*.

[*Osmyn* ascending from the Tomb.

Osm. Who calls that wretched Thing that was *Alphonso*?

21

Alm. Angels, and all the Host of Heaven, support me!

Osm. Whence is that Voice, whose Shrilness, from the Grave,
And growing to his dead Father's Shroud, roots up
Alphonso?

Alm. Mercy and Providence! O speak to it,
Speak to it quickly, quickly; speak to me,
Comfort me, help me, hold me, hide me, hide me,
Leonora, in thy Bosom, from the Light,
And from my Eyes.

Osm. Amazement and Illusion! Rivet me
To Earth, and nail me where I stand, ye Powers,

[*Coming forward.*

That motionless I may be still deceiv'd.
Let me not stir, nor breath, lest I dissolve
That tender, lovely Form of painted Air,
So like *Almeria.* Ha! it sinks, it falls;
I'll catch it e'er it goes, and grasp her Shade.
'Tis Life! 'tis warm! 'tis she! 'tis she her self!
Nor Dead, nor Shade, but breathing and alive!
It is *Almeria!* 'tis my Wife!

Enter Heli.

Leo. O Heaven unfold these Wonders!
Alas, she stirs not yet, nor lifts her Eyes;
He too is fainting—Help me, help me, Stranger,
Who e'er thou art, and lend thy Hand to raise
These Bodies.

Hel. By Heav'n 'tis he, and with—ha! *Almeria!*
Almeria! O Miracle of Happiness!
O Joy unhop'd for, does *Almeria* live!

Osm. Where is she?
Let me behold and touch her, and be sure
'Tis she; shew me her Face, and let me feel
Her Lips with mine—'Tis she, I'm not deceiv'd;
I taste her Breath, I warm'd her and am warm'd.
Look up, *Almeria,* bless me with thy Eyes;
Look on thy Love, thy Lover, and thy Husband,
Look on *Alphonso.*

Alm. I've sworn I'll not wed *Garcia;* why d'ye force me?
Is this a Father?

Osm. Thy Father is not here, nor *Garcia:* I am
Neither, nor what I seem, but thy *Alphonso.*
Wilt thou not know me? Hast thou then forgot me?
Hast thou thy Eyes, yet can'st not see *Alphonso?*

Am I so alter'd, or art thou so chang'd,
That seeing my Disguise, thou seest not me?

Alm. It is, it is *Alphonso,* 'tis his Face,
His Voice, I know him now, I know him all.
O take me to thy Arms, and bear me hence,
Back to the Bottom of the boundless Deep,
To Seas beneath, where thou so long hast dwelt.
O how hast thou return'd? How hast thou charm'd
The wildness of the Waves and Rocks to this?
That thus relenting, they have giv'n thee back
To Earth, to Light and Life, to Love and me.

Osm. O I'll not ask, nor answer how, or why,
We both have backward trod the Paths of Fate,
To meet again in Life; to know I have thee,
Is knowing more than any Circumstance
Or Means by which I have thee—
To fold thee thus, to press thy balmy Lips,
And gaze upon thy Eyes, is so much Joy,
I have not leisure to reflect, or know,
Or trifle Time in thinking.

Alm. Let me look on thee, yet a little more.

Osm. What would'st thou? thou dost put me from thee.

Alm. Yes.

Osm. Why? what dost thou mean? why dost thou gaze so?

Alm. I know not, 'tis to see thy Face, I think—
It is too much! too much to bear and live!
To see him thus again is such Profusion
Of Delight, I cannot bear it—I shall
Be mad—I cannot be transported thus.

Osm. Thou Excellence, thou Joy, thou Heav'n of Love!

Alm. Where hast thou been? and how art thou alive?
How is all this? All-powerful Heav'n, what are we!
O my strain'd Heart—let me behold thee,
For I weep to see thee—Art thou not paler?
Much, much, alas; how thou art chang'd!

Osm. Not in my Love.

Alm. No, no, thy Griefs have done this to thee.
Thou hast wept much, *Alphonso;* and, I fear,
Too much lamented me.

Osm. Wrong not my Love, to say too much.
No more, my Life; talk not of Tears or Grief;
Affliction is no more, now thou art found.
Why dost thou weep, and hold thee from my Arms,

My Arms which ake to fold thee fast, and grow
To thee with twining? Come, come to my Heart.

Alm. I will, for I should never look enough.
They would have marry'd me; but I had sworn
To Heav'n and thee, and sooner wou'd have dy'd—

Osm. Perfection of all Truth!

Alm. Indeed I wou'd—Nay, I wou'd tell thee all,
If I cou'd speak; how I have mourn'd and pray'd;
For I have pray'd to thee as to a Saint:
And thou hast heard my Prayer; for thou art come
To my Distress, to my Despair, which Heav'n
Without thee could not cure.

Osm. Grant me but Life, good Heaven, but length of Days,
To pay some Part, some little of this Debt,
This countless Sum of Tenderness and Love,
For which I stand engag'd to this All-excellence:
Then bear me in a Whirlwind to my Fate,
Snatch me from Life, and cut me short unwarn'd;
Then, then 'twill be enough—I shall be Old,
I shall have liv'd beyond all *Aera*'s then
Of yet unmeasur'd Time; when I have made
This exquisite, amazing Goodness,
Some Recompence of Love and matchless Truth.

Alm. 'Tis more than Recompence, to see thy Face:
If Heav'n is greater Joy it is no Happiness,
For 'tis not to be born—What shall I say?
I have a thousand Things to know, and ask,
And speak—That thou art here, beyond all Hope,
All Thought; that all at once thou art before me,
And with such Suddenness hast hit my Sight,
Is such Surprize, such Mystery, such Extasie,
As hurries all my Soul, and dozes my weak Sense.
Sure from thy Father's Tomb thou didst arise!

Osm. I did, and thou didst call me.

Alm. How cam'st thou there? Wert thou alone?

Osm. I was, and lying on my Father's Lead,
When broken Ecchoes of a distant Voice
Disturb'd the Sacred Silence of the Vault,
In Murmurs round my Head. I rose and listened,
And thought I heard thy Spirit call *Alphonso*;
I thought I saw thee too; but O, I thought not
I indeed shou'd see thee—

Alm. But still, how cam'st thee hither? how thus?—Ha!
What's he, that like thy self is started here

24

E'er seen?

Osm. Where? ha! what do I see? *Antonio* here?
My Friend too safe!

Hel. Most happily, in finding you thus bless'd.

Alm. More Miracles! *Antonio* too escap'd!

Osm. And twice escap'd, both from the Wreck of Seas
And Rage of War: For in the Fight I saw
Him fall.

Hel. But fell unhurt, a Prisoner as your self,
And as your self made free; hither I came
To seek you, where I knew your Grief would lead you,
To lament *Anselmo.*—

Osm. There are no Wonders, or else all is Wonder.

Hel. I saw you on the Ground, and rais'd you up.
I saw *Almeria*—

Osm. I saw her too, and therefore saw not thee.

Alm. Nor I, nor could I, for my Eyes were yours.

Osm. What means the Bounty of All-gracious Heav'n,
That thus with open Hand it scatters Good,
As in a waste of Mercy?
Where will this end! but Heav'n is Infinite
In all, and can continue to bestow,
When scanty Number shall be spent in telling.

Leo. Or I'm deceiv'd, or I beheld the Glimpse
Of two in shining Habits cross the Isle,
And bending this way.

Alm. Sure I have dreamt, if we must part so soon.

Osm. I wish our parting were a Dream, or we
Could sleep 'till we again were met.

Hel. *Zara* with *Selim,* Sir, I saw and know 'em:
You must be quick, for Love will lend her Wings.

Alm. What Love? who is she?

Osm. She's the Reverse of thee; she's my Unhappiness.
Harbour no Thought that may disturb thy Peace;
But gently take thy self away, lest she
Should come and see the straining of my Eyes
To follow thee. I'll think how we may meet
To part no more; my Friend will tell thee all;
How I escap'd, how I am here, and thus;
How I'm not call'd *Alphonso,* now, but *Osmyn;*
And he *Heli.* All, all he will unfold.

Alm. Sure we shall meet again.

Osm. We shall; we part not but to meet again.
Gladness and Warmth of ever-kindling Love
Dwell with thee, and revive thy Heart in Absence.

[Ex. *Alm. Leon.* and *Heli.*

Yet I behold her—Now no more.
Turn your Lights inward, Eyes, and look
Upon my Thought; so shall you still behold her.
It wonnot be; O, impotence of Sight!
Mechanick Sense, which to exterior Objects
Owest thy Faculty.—
Not seeing of Election, but Necessity.
Thus do our Eyes, like common Mirrours,
Successively reflect succeeding Images;
Not what they would, but must; a Star, or Toad:
Just as the Hand of Chance administers.
Not so the Mind, whose undetermin'd View
Revolves, and to the present adds the past:
Essaying further to Futurity;
But that in vain. I have *Almeria* here
At once, as I have seen her often;
I'll muse on that, lest I exceed in thinking.

Enter *Zara* attended by *Selim.*

Zara. See where he stands, folded and fix'd to Earth,
Stiff'ning in Thought; a Statue among Statues.
Why, cruel *Osmyn*, dost thou fly me thus?
Is it well done? Is this then the Return
For Fame, for Honour, and for Empire lost?
But what is loss of Honour, Fame and Empire?
Is this the Recompence of Love?
Why dost thou leave my Eyes, and fly my Arms,
To find this place of Horror and Obscurity?
Am I more loathsome to thee than the Grave,
That thou dost seek to shield thee there, and shun
My Love? But to the Grave I'll follow thee—
He looks not, minds not, hears not; barbarous Man,
Am I neglected thus? Am I despis'd?
Not heard! Ungrateful *Osmyn.*

Osm. Ha, *Zara!*

Zara. Yes, Traitor; *Zara*, lost, abandon'd *Zara*,
Is a regardless Suppliant, now, to *Osmyn.*
The Slave, the Wretch that she redeem'd from Death,
Disdains to listen now, or look on *Zara.*

Osm. Far be the Guilt of such Reproaches from me;
Lost in my self, and blinded by my Thoughts,

26

I saw you not.

Zara. Now then you see me—
But with such dumb and thankless Eyes you look,
Better I was unseen, than seen thus coldly.

Osm. What would you from a Wretch that came to mourn;
And only for his Sorrows chose this Solitude?
Look round; Joy is not here, nor Chearfulness.
You have pursu'd Misfortune to its Dwelling,
Yet look for Gaiety and Gladness there.

Zara. Inhuman! why, why dost thou wrack me thus?
And with Perverseness, from the Purpose, answer?
What is't to me, this House of Misery?
What Joy do I require? If thou dost mourn,
I come to mourn with thee; to share thy Griefs,
And give thee in Exchange my Love.

Osm. O that's the greatest Grief—I am so poor,
I have not wherewithal to give again.

Zara. Thou hast a Heart, though 'tis a Savage one;
Give it me as it is; I ask no more
For all I've done, and all I have endur'd:
For saving thee, when I beheld thee first,
Driven by the Tide upon my Country's Coast,
Pale and expiring, drench'd in Briny Waves,
Thou and thy Friend, 'till my Compassion found thee;
Compassion! scarce will it own that Name, so soon,
So quickly was it Love; for thou wert God-like
Ev'n then. Kneeling on Earth, I loos'd my Hair,
And with it dry'd thy wat'ry Cheeks; chasing
Thy Temples, 'till reviving Blood arose,
And like the Morn Vermilion'd o'er thy Face.
O Heav'n! how did my Heart rejoice and ake,
When I beheld the Day-break of thy Eyes,
And felt the Balm of thy respiring Lips!

Osm. O call not to my Mind what you have done,
It sets a Debt of that Account before me,
Which shews me Bankrupt even in Hopes.

Zara. The faithful *Selim,* and my Women know
The Dangers which I tempted to conceal you.
You know how I abus'd the credulous King;
What Arts I us'd to make you pass on him,
When he receiv'd you as the Prince of *Fez;*
And as my Kinsman, honour'd and advanc'd you.
O, why do I relate what I have done?
What did I not? Was't not for you this War
Commenc'd? Not knowing who you were, nor why

You hated *Manuel,* I urg'd my Husband
On to this Invasion; where he was lost;
Where all is lost, and I am made a Slave.
Look on me now, from Empire fall'n to Slavery;
Think on my Suff'rings first, then look on me;
Think on the Cause of all, then view thy self:
Reflect on *Osmyn,* and then look on *Zara,*
The fall'n, the lost, the Captive *Zara.*
What then is *Osmyn?*

Osm. A fatal Wretch—a huge stupendious Ruin,
That tumbling on its Prop, crush'd all beneath,
And bore contiguous Palaces to Earth.

Zara. Yet thus, thus fall'n, thus levell'd with the vilest,
If I have gain'd thy Love, 'tis glorious Ruin;
Ruin! 'tis still to reign, and to be more
A Queen; for what are Riches, Empire, Power,
But larger Means to gratifie the Will?
The Steps on which we tread, to rise, and reach
Our Wish; and that obtain'd, down with the Scaffolding
Of Sceptres, Crowns, and Thrones; they've serv'd their End,
And are, like Lumber, to be left and scorn'd.

Osm. Why was I made the Instrument, to throw
In Bonds the Frame of this exalted Mind?

Zara. We may be free; the Conqueror is mine;
In Chains unseen I hold him by the Heart,
And can unwind or strain him as I please.
Give me thy Love, I'll give thee Liberty.

Osm. In vain you offer, and in vain require
What neither can bestow. Set free your self,
And leave a Slave the Wretch that would be so.

Zara. Thou canst not mean so poorly as thou talk'st.

Osm. Alas, you know me not.

Zara. Not who thou art;
But what, this last Ingratitude declares,
This groveling Baseness—Thou say'st true, I know
Thee not, for what thou art yet wants a Name:
But something so unworthy, and so vile,
That to have lov'd thee makes me yet more lost,
Than all the Malice of my other Fate.
Traitor, Monster, cold and perfidious Slave;
A Slave, not daring to be free! nor dares
To love above him, for 'tis dangerous:
'Tis that, I know; for thou dost look, with Eyes
Sparkling Desire, and trembling to possess.

I know my Charms have reach'd thy very Soul,
And thrill'd thee through with darted Fires; but thou
Dost fear so much, thou dar'st not wish. The King!
There, there's the dreadful Sound, the King's thy Rival!

Selim. Madam, the King is here.

Zara. As I could wish; by Heav'n I'll be reveng'd.

                     Enter the King, *Perez,* and Attendants.

King. Why does the Fairest of her Kind withdraw
Her Shining from the Day, to gild this Scene
Of Death and Night? Ha! what Disorder's this?
Somewhat I heard of King and Rival mention'd.
What's he that dares be Rival to the King?
Or lift his Eyes to like, where I adore?

Zara. There, he; your Prisoner, and that was my Slave.

King. How? Better than my Hopes? Does she accuse him?
[*Aside.*

Zara. Am I become so low by my Captivity,
And do your Arms so lessen what they conquer,
That *Zara* must be made the Sport of Slaves?
And shall the Wretch, whom yester Sun beheld
Waiting my Nod, the Creature of my Lord
And me, presume to Day to plead audacious Love,
And build bold Hopes on my dejected Fate?

King. Better for him to tempt the Rage of Heav'n,
And wrench the Bolt red-hissing from the Hand
Of him that thunders, than but think that Insolence.
'Tis daring for a God. Hence, to the Wheel
With that *Ixion,* who aspires to hold
Divinity embrac'd; to Whips and Prisons
Drag him with speed, and rid me of his Face.
[Guards carry off *Osmyn.*

Zara. Compassion led me to bemoan his State,
Whose former Faith had merited much more:
And through my Hopes in you, I promis'd Freedom
From his Chains; thence sprung his Insolence,
And what was Charity, he constru'd Love.

King. Enough; his Punishment be what you please.
But let me lead you from this Place of Sorrow,
To one, where young Delights attend; and Joys
Yet new, unborn, and blooming in the Bud,
That wait to be full-blown at your Approach,
And spread like Roses to the Morning Sun:
Where ev'ry Hour shall roll in circling Joys,

And Love shall wing the tedious-wasting Day.
Life without Love is Load; and Time stands still:
What we refuse to him, to Death we give;
And then, then only, when we love, we live.

[Ex. Omnes.

Act III.

Scene I.

A Prison.

Enter *Osmyn* alone, with a Paper.

Osm. BUT now, and I was clos'd within the Tomb
That holds my Father's Ashes; and but now,
Where he was Pris'ner I am too imprison'd.
Sure 'tis the Hand of Heav'n that leads me thus,
And for some Purpose points out these Remembrances.
In a dark Corner of my Cell I found
This Paper, what it is this Light will show.

Reading.

If my Alphonso—Ha!
If my Alphonso *live, restore him, Heav'n;*
Give me more Weight, crush my declining Years
With Bolts, with Chains, Imprisonment and Want;
But bless my Son, visit not him for me.

It is his-Hand; this was his Pray'r—yet more:

Reading.

Let ev'ry Hair, which Sorrow by the Roots
Tears from my hoary and devoted Head,
Be doubled in thy Mercies to my Son:
Not for my self, but him, hear me, All-gracious—

'Tis wanting what should follow—*Heav'n* shou'd follow,
But 'tis torn off—Why shou'd that Word alone
Be torn from his Petition? 'Twas to Heav'n,
But Heav'n was deaf, Heav'n heard him not; but thus,
Thus as the Name of Heav'n from this is torn,
So did it tear the Ears of Mercy from
His Voice, shutting the Gates of Pray'r against him.
If Piety be thus debarr'd Access
On high, and of good Men the very best
Is singled out to bleed, and bear the Scourge,
What is Reward? or what is Punishment?
But who shall dare to tax Eternal Justice!
Yet I may think—I may, I must; for Thought
Precedes the Will to think, and Error lives
E'er Reason can be born: Reason, the Power
To guess at Right and Wrong; the twinkling Lamp
Of wand'ring Life, that winks and wakes by turns,
Fooling the Follower, betwixt Shade and Shining.
What Noise! Who's there? my Friend! How cam'st thou hither?

Enter *Heli.*

Hel. The Time's too precious to be spent in telling;
The Captain, influenc'd by *Almeria*'s Power,
Gave Order to the Guards for my Admittance.

Osm. How does *Almeria?* But I know, she is
As I am. Tell me, may I hope to see her?

Hel. You may; anon, at Midnight, when the King
Is gone to Rest, and *Garcia* is retir'd,
(Who takes the Privilege to visit late,
Presuming on a Bridegroom's Right) she'll come.

Osm. She'll come; 'tis what I wish, yet what I fear.
She'll come, but whither, and to whom? O Heav'n!
To a vile Prison, and a captiv'd Wretch;
To one, whom had she never known she had
Been happy: Why, why was that Heav'nly Creature
Abandon'd o'er to love what Heav'n forsakes?
Why does she follow, with unwearied Steps,
One, who has tir'd Misfortune with pursuing?
One, driv'n about the World like blasted Leaves
And Chaff, the Sport of adverse Winds; 'till late
At length, imprison'd in some Cleft of Rock,
Or Earth, it rests, and rots to silent Dust.

Hel. Have Hopes, and hear the Voice of better Fate.
I've learn'd there are Disorders ripe for Mutiny
Among the Troops, who thought to share the Plunder,
Which *Manuel* to his own Use and Avarice
Converts. This News has reach'd *Valentia*'s Frontiers;
Where many of your Subjects, long oppress'd
With Tyranny and grievous Impositions,
Are risen in Arms, and call for Chiefs to head
And lead 'em, to regain their Liberty
And Native Rights.

Osm. By Heav'n thou'st rouz'd me from my Lethargy.
The Spirit which was deaf to my own Wrongs,
Deaf to Revenge, and the loud Cries of my
Dead Father's Blood; nay, which refus'd to hear
The piercing Sighs and Murmurs of my Love
Yet unenjoy'd; what not *Almeria* could
Revive, or raise, my Peoples Voice has waken'd.
O my *Antonio,* I am all on Fire,
My Soul is up in Arms, ready to charge
And bear amidst the Foe, with conqu'ring Troops.
I hear 'em call to lead 'em on to Liberty,
To Victory; their Shouts and Clamours rend
My Ears, and reach the Heav'ns; where is the King?
Where is *Alphonso?* ha! where? where indeed?
O I could tear and burst the Strings of Life,

To break these Chains. Off, off, ye Stains of Royalty.
Off Slavery. O curse! that I alone
Can beat and flutter in my Cage, when I
Would soar, and stoop at Victory beneath.

Hel. Our Posture of Affairs, and scanty Time,
My Lord, require you should compose your self,
And think on what we may reduce to practice.
Zara, the Cause of your Restraint, may be
The Means of Liberty restor'd. That gain'd,
Occasion will not fail to point out Ways
For your Escape. Mean time, I've thought already
With Speed and Safety, to convey my self
Where not far off some Male-Contents hold Council
Nightly; hating this Tyrant; some, who love
Anselmo's Memory, and will, no doubt,
When they shall know you live, assist your Cause.

Osm. My Friend and Counsellor, as thou think'st fit,
So do. I will with Patience wait my Fortune.

Hel. When *Zara* comes, abate of your Aversion.

Osm. I hate her not, nor can dissemble Love:
But as I may, I'll do. I have a Paper
Which I would shew thee, Friend, but that the Sight
Would hold thee here, and clog thy Expedition.
Within I found it, by my Father's Hand
'Twas writ; a Pray'r for me, wherein appears
Paternal Love prevailing o'er his Sorrows;
Such Sanctity, such Tenderness, so mix'd
With Grief, as wou'd draw Tears from Inhumanity.

Hel. The Care of Providence sure left it there,
To arm your Mind with Hope. Such Piety
Was never heard in vain: Heav'n has in Store
For you, those Blessings it with-held from him.
In that Assurance live; which Time, I hope,
And our next Meeting will confirm.

Osm. Farewel,
My Friend, the Good thou dost deserve attend thee.

[Ex. *Heli.*

I've been to blame, and question'd with Impiety
The Care of Heav'n. Not so my Father bore
More Anxious Grief. This shou'd have better taught me;
This Lesson, in some Hour of Inspiration,
By him set down; when his pure Thoughts were born,
Like Fumes of Sacred Incense, o'er the Clouds,
And wafted thence, on Angels Wings, thro' Ways
Of Light to the bright Source of all. There, in

33

The Book of Prescience, he beheld this Day;
And waking to the World and Mortal Sense,
Left this Example of his Resignation,
This his last Legacy to me, which I
Will treasure here; more worth than Diadems,
Or all extended Rule of Regal Pow'r.

Enter Zara Veil'd.

What Brightness breaks upon me thus thro' Shades,
And promises a Day to this dark Dwelling!
Is it my Love?—

Zara. O that thy Heart had taught

[*Lifting her Veil.*

Thy Tongue that Saying.

Osm. Zara! I'm betray'd
By my Surprize.

Zara. What, does my Face displease thee?
That having seen it, thou dost turn thy Eyes
Away, as from Deformity and Horror.
If so, this Sable Curtain shall again
Be drawn, and I will stand before thee seeing,
And unseen. Is it my Love? ask again
That Question, speak again in that soft Voice,
And look again with Wishes in thy Eyes.
O no, thou can'st not, for thou seest me now,
As she, whose Savage Breast has been the Cause
Of these thy Wrongs; as she, whose barbarous Rage
Has loaden thee with Chains and galling Irons:
Well dost thou scorn me, and upbraid my Falseness;
Cou'd one that lov'd thus torture what she lov'd?
No, no, it must be Hatred, dire Revenge
And Detestation, that cou'd use thee thus.
So thou dost think; then do but tell me so;
Tell me, and thou shalt see how I'll revenge
Thee on this false one, how I'll stab and tear
This Heart of Flint 'till it shall bleed; and thou
Shalt weep for mine, forgetting thy own Miseries.

Osm. You wrong me, beauteous *Zara*, to believe
I bear my Fortunes with so low a Mind,
As still to meditate Revenge on all
Whom Chance, or Fate working by secret Causes,
Has made perforce subservient to that End
The Heav'nly Pow'rs allot me; no, not you,
But Destiny and inauspicious Stars
Have cast me down to this low Being: Or,

34

Granting you had, from you I have deserv'd it.

Zara. Can'st thou forgive me then? wilt thou believe
So kindly of my Fault, to call it Madness?
O, give that Madness yet a milder Name,
And call it Passion; then, be still more kind,
And call that Passion Love.

Osm. Give it a Name,
Or Being as you please, such I will think it.

Zara. O thou dost wound me more with this thy Goodness,
Than e'er thou cou'dst with bitterest Reproaches;
Thy Anger cou'd not pierce thus to my Heart.

Osm. Yet I could wish—

Zara. Haste me to know it, what?

Osm. That at this Time I had not been this Thing.

Zara. What Thing?

Osm. This Slave.

Zara. O Heav'n! my Fears interpret
This thy Silence; somewhat of high Concern,
Long fashioning within thy labouring Mind,
And now just ripe for Birth, my Rage has ruin'd.
Have I done this? Tell me, am I so curs'd?

Osm. Time may have still one fated Hour to come,
Which wing'd with Liberty, might overtake
Occasion past.

Zara. Swift as Occasion, I
My self will flie; and earlier than the Morn
Wake thee to Freedom. Now 'tis late; and yet
Some News few Minutes past arriv'd, which seem'd
To shake the Temper of the King—who knows
What racking Cares disease a Monarch's Bed?
Or Love, that late at Night still lights his Lamp,
And strikes his Rays thro' dusk and folded Lids,
Forbidding Rest, may stretch his Eyes awake,
And force their Balls abroad at this dead Hour.
I'll try.

Osm. I have not merited this Grace;
Nor, should my secret Purpose take Effect,
Can I repay, as you require, such Benefits.

Zara. Thou canst not owe me more, nor have I more
To give, than I've already lost. But as
The present Form of our Engagements rests,
Thou hast the Wrong, 'till I redeem thee hence,
That done, I leave thy Justice to return

My Love. Adieu.

[Exit *Zara*.

Osm. This Woman has a Soul
Of God-like Mould, intrepid and commanding,
And challenges, in spight of me, my best
Esteem; to this she's fair, few more can boast
Of Personal Charms, or with less Vanity
Might hope to captivate the Hearts of Kings.
But she has Passions which out-strip the Wind,
And tear her Virtues up, as Tempests root
The Sea. I fear when she shall know the Truth,
Some swift and dire Event of her blind Rage
Will make all fatal. But behold, she comes
For whom I fear, to shield me from my Fears.

Enter *Almeria*.

The Cause and Comfort of my boding Heart,
My Life, my Health, my Liberty, my All,
How shall I welcome thee to this sad Place?
How speak to thee the Words of Joy and Transport?
How run into thy Arms, with-held by Fetters;
Or take thee into mine, thus manacled
And pinion'd like a Thief or Murderer?
Shall I not hurt or bruise thy tender Body,
And stain thy Bosom with the Rust of these
Rude Irons? Must I meet thee thus, *Almeria?*

Alm. Thus, thus; we parted, thus to meet again.
Thou told'st me thou would'st think how we might meet
To part no more—Now we will part no more,
For these thy Chains, or Death, shall join us ever.

Osm. Hard Means to ratify that Word!—O Cruelty!
That ever I should think beholding thee
A Torture!—yet, such is the bleeding Anguish
Of my Heart, to see thy Sufferings—O Heav'n!
That I cou'd almost turn my Eyes away,
Or wish thee from my Sight.

Alm. O say not so;
Tho' 'tis because thou lov'st me. Do not say,
On any Terms, that thou dost wish me from thee.
No, no, 'tis better thus, that we together
Feed on each other's Heart, devour our Woes
With mutual Appetite; and mingling in
One Cup the common Stream of both our Eyes,
Drink bitter Draughts, with never-slacking Thirst.
Thus better, than for any Cause to part.
What dost thou think? Look not so tenderly

36

Upon me—speak, and take me in thy Arms—
Thou canst not! thy poor Arms are bound, and strive
In vain with the remorseless Chains, which gnaw
And eat into thy Flesh, festring thy Limbs
With rankling Rust.

Osm. Oh! O—

Alm. Give me that Sigh.
Why dost thou heave, and stifle in thy Griefs?
Thy Heart will burst, thy Eyes look red and start;
Give thy Soul way, and tell me thy dark Thought.

Osm. For this World's Rule, I wou'd not wound thy Breast
With such a Dagger as then stuck my Heart.

Alm. Why? why? To know it, cannot wound me more,
Than knowing thou hast felt it. Tell it me.
—Thou giv'st me Pain with too much Tenderness!

Osm. And thy excessive Love distracts my Sense!
O could'st thou be less killing, soft or kind,
Grief would not double thus his Darts against me.

Alm. Thou dost me Wrong, and Grief too robs my Heart,
If there he shoot not ev'ry other Shaft;
Thy second self shou'd feel each other Wound,
And Woe shou'd be in equal Portions dealt.
I am thy Wife—

Osm. O thou hast search'd too deep:
There, there I bleed; there pull the cruel Cords,
That strain my cracking Nerves; Engines and Wheels,
That Piece-meal grind, are Beds of Down and Balm
To that Soul-racking Thought.

Alm. Then I am curs'd
Indeed, if that be so; if I'm thy Torment
Kill me, kill me then, dash me with thy Chains,
Tread on me, spurn me: Am I the Bosom-Snake,
That sucks thy warm Life-Blood, and gnaws thy Heart?
O that thy Words had force to break those Bonds,
As they have strength to tear this Heart in sunder;
So should'st thou be at large from all Oppression.
Am I, am I of all thy Woes the worst?

Osm. My all of Bliss, my everlasting Life,
Soul of my Soul, and End of all my Wishes,
Why dost thou thus unman me with thy Words,
And melt me down to mingle with thy Weepings?
What dost thou ask? why dost thou talk thus piercingly?
Thy Sorrows have disturb'd thy Peace of Mind,
And thou dost speak of Miseries impossible.

Alm. Didst thou not say, that Racks and Wheels were Balm,
And Beds of Ease, to thinking me thy Wife?

Osm. No, no; nor should the subtlest Pains that Hell,
Or Hell-born Malice can invent, extort
A Wish or Thought from me, to have thee other.
But thou wilt know what harrows up my Heart:
Thou art my Wife—nay, thou art yet my Bride!
The Sacred Union of Connubial Love
Yet unaccomplish'd; his mysterious Rites
Delay'd; nor has our Hymenial Torch
Yet lighted up his last most grateful Sacrifice;
But dash'd with Rain from Eyes, and swail'd with Sighs,
Burns dim, and glimmers with expiring Light.
Is this dark Cell a Temple for that God?
Or this vile Earth an Altar for such Off'rings?
This Den for Slaves, this Dungeon damp'd with Woes;
Is this our Marriage-Bed! Are these our Joys!
Is this to call thee mine? O hold my Heart:
To call thee mine? Yes; thus, ev'n thus, to call
Thee mine, were Comfort, Joy, extreamest Extasie.
But O thou art not mine, not ev'n in Misery;
And 'tis deny'd to me to be so bless'd,
As to be wretched with thee.

Alm. No; not that
The extreamest Malice of our Fate can hinder:
That still is left us, and on that we'll feed,
As on the Leavings of Calamity.
There we will feast, and smile on past Distress,
And hug, in scorn of it, our mutual Ruin.

Osm. O thou dost talk, my Love, as one resolv'd,
Because not knowing Danger. But look forward;
Think on to Morrow, when thou shalt be torn
From these weak, struggling, unextended Arms;
Think how my Heart will heave, and Eyes will strain,
To grasp and reach what is deny'd my Hands:
Think how the Blood will start, and Tears will gush
To follow thee, my separating Soul.
Think how I am, when thou shalt wed with *Garcia!*
Then will I smear these Walls with Blood, dash my
Disfigur'd Face, and rive my clotted Hair,
Break on the Ground my throbbing Breast,
And grovel with gash'd Hands to scratch a Grave,
Stripping my Nails, to tear this Pavement up,
And bury me alive; where I will bite the Ground
'Till gorg'd with suffocating Earth.

Alm. O dismal Cruel! heart-breaking Horror!

Osm. Then *Garcia* shall lie panting on thy Bosom,
Luxurious, revelling amidst thy Charms;
And thou perforce must yield, and aid his Transport.
Hell! Hell! have I not Cause to rage and rave?
What are all Racks, and Wheels, and Whips to this?
Are they not soothing Softness, sinking Ease,
And wafting Air to this? O my *Almeria,*
What do the Damn'd endure, but to despair,
But knowing Heav'n, to know it lost for ever?

Alm. O, I am struck; thy Words are Bolts of Ice,
Which shot into my Breast, now melt and chill me.
I chatter, shake, and faint with thrilling Fears.
No, hold me not—O, let us not support,
But sink each other, lower yet, down, down,
Where levell'd low, no more we'll lift our Eyes,
But prone, and dumb, rot the firm Face of Earth
With Rivers of incessant scalding Rain.

Enter Zara, Perez and Selim.

Zara. Somewhat of weight to me requires his Freedom.
Dare you dispute the King's Command? Behold
The Royal Signet.

Perez. I obey; yet beg
Your Majesty one Moment to defer
Your ent'ring, 'till the Princess is return'd
From visiting the Noble Prisoner.

[Exit Perez.

Zara. Ha!
What saist thou?

Osm. We are lost! undone! discover'd!
Retire, my Life, with speed—Alas, we're seen!
Speak of Compassion, let her hear you speak
Of interceeding for me with the King;
Say somewhat quickly to conceal our Loves,
If possible.—

Alm. —I cannot speak.

Osm. Let me
Conduct you forth, as not perceiving her,
But 'till she's gone; then bless me thus again.

Zara. Trembling and weeping as he leads her forth!
Confusion in his Face, and Grief in hers!
'Tis plain, I've been abus'd—Death and Destruction!
How shall I search into this Mystery?
The bluest Blast of Pestilential Air
Strike, damp, deaden her Charms, and kill his Eyes;

39

Perdition catch 'em both, and Ruin part 'em

Osm. This Charity to one unknown, and in
Distress, Heav'n will repay; all Thanks are poor.

[Exit *Almeria.*

Zara. Damn'd, damn'd Dissembler! Yet I will be calm,
Choak in my Rage, and know the utmost depth
Of this Deceiver—You seem much surpriz'd.

Osm. At your Return so soon and unexpected!

Zara. And so unwish'd, unwanted too it seems.
Confusion! yet I will contain my self.
You're grown a Favourite since last we parted;
Perhaps I'm Sawcy and Intruding—

Osm. —Madam!

Zara. I did not know the Princess Favourite;
Your Pardon, Sir—mistake me not; you think
I'm angry; you're deceiv'd. I came to set
You free: But shall return much better pleas'd,
To find you have an Interest superior.

Osm. You do not come to mock my Miseries?

Zara. I do.

Osm. I could at this time spare your Mirth.

Zara. I know thou cou'dst, but I'm not often pleas'd,
And will indulge it now. What Miseries?
Who would not be thus happily confin'd,
To be the Care of weeping Majesty?
To have contending Queens, at dead of Night
Forsake their Down, to wake with wat'ry Eyes,
And watch like Tapers o'er your Hours of Rest.
O Curse! I cannot hold.—

Osm. Come, 'tis much.

Zara. Villain!

Osm. How, Madam!

Zara. Thou shalt die.

Osm. I thank you.

Zara. Thou ly'st; for now I know for whom thou'dst live.

Osm. Then you may know for whom I'd die.

Zara. Hell! Hell!
Yet I'll be calm—Dark and unknown Betrayer!
But now the Dawn begins, and the slow Hand
Of Fate is stretch'd to draw the Veil, and leave
Thee bare, the naked Mark of Publick View.

40

Osm. You may be still deceiv'd; 'tis in my Pow'r.

Zara. Ha!
Who waits there?

Enter Perez.

As you'll answer it, take heed
This Slave commit no Violence upon
Himself. I've been deceiv'd. The Publick Safety
Requires he should be more confin'd; and none,
No not the Princes self, permitted to
Confer with him. I'll quit you to the King.
Vile and ingrate! too late thou shalt repent
The base Injustice thou hast done my Love:
Yes, thou shalt know, spite of thy past Distress,
And all those Ills which thou so long hast mourn'd;
Heav'n has no Rage, like Love to Hatred turn'd,
Nor Hell a Fury, like a Woman scorn'd.

[Exeunt Omnes.

Act IV.

Scene I.

A Room of State.

Enter *Zara* and *Selim*.

Zara. THOU hast already rack'd me with thy Stay;
Therefore require me not to ask thee twice:
Reply at once to all. What is concluded?

Selim. Your Accusation highly has incens'd
The King, and were alone enough to urge
The Fate of *Osmyn;* but to that, fresh News
Is since arriv'd, of more revolted Troops.
'Tis certain *Heli* too is fled, and with him
(Which breeds Amazement and Distraction) some
Who bore high Offices of Weight and Trust,
Both in the State and Army. This confirms
The King, in full Belief of all you told him,
Concerning *Osmyn's* corresponding with
The Heads of those who first began the Mutiny.
Wherefore a Warrant for his Death is sign'd;
And Order given for Publick Execution.

Zara. Ha! haste thee! fly, prevent his Fate and mine;
Find out the King, tell him I have of Weight
More than his Crown t'impart e'er *Osmyn* die.

Selim. It needs not, for the King will strait be here,
And as to your Revenge, not his own Int'rest,
Pretend to Sacrifice the Life of *Osmyn.*

Zara. What shall I say? Invent; contrive, advise
Somewhat to blind the King, and save his Life
In whom I live. Spite of my Rage and Pride,
I am a Woman, and a Lover still.
O! 'tis more Grief but to suppose his Death,
Than still to meet the Rigour of his Scorn.
From my Despair my Anger had its Source;
When he is dead I must despair for ever.
For ever! that's Despair—it was Distrust
Before; Distrust will ever be in Love,
And Anger in Distrust, both short-liv'd Pains.
But in Despair, and ever-during Death,
No Term, no Bound, but Infinite of Woe.
O Torment, but to think! what then to bear?
Not to be born—Devise the Means to shun it,
Quick; or, by Heav'n, this Dagger drinks thy Blood.

Selim. My Life is yours, nor wish I to preserve it,

But to serve you. I have already thought.

Zara. Forgive my Rage; I know thy Love and Truth.
But say, what's to be done? or when, or how
Shall I prevent, or stop th' approaching Danger?

Selim. You must still seem most resolute and fix'd
On *Osmyn*'s Death; too quick a Change of Mercy
Might breed Suspicion of the Cause. Advise,
That Execution may be done in private.

Zara. On what Pretence?

Selim. Your own Request's enough.
However, for a Colour, tell him, you
Have Cause to fear his Guards may be corrupted,
And some of them bought off to *Osmyn*'s Int'rest;
Who, at the Place of Execution, will
Attempt to force his way for an Escape.
The State of things will countenance all Suspicions
Then offer to the King to have him strangl'd
In secret, by your Mutes; and get an Order,
That none but Mutes may have Admittance to him.
I can no more, the King is here. Obtain
This Grant—and I'll acquaint you with the rest.

Enter King, Gonsalez, Garcia, Perez

King. Bear to the Dungeon those Rebellious Slaves,
Th'ignoble Currs, that yelp to fill the Cry,
And spend their Mouths in barking Tyranny.
But for their Leaders, *Sancho* and *Ramirez,*
Let'em be led away to present Death.
Perez, see it perform'd.

Gons. Might I presume,
Their Execution better were deferr'd,
'Till *Osmyn* die. Mean time we may learn more
Of this Conspiracy.

King. Then be it so.
Stay, Soldier; they shall suffer with the *Moor.*
Are none return'd of those who follow'd *Heli?*

Gons. None, Sir. Some Papers have been since discover'd
In *Roderigo*'s House, who fled with him,
Which seem to intimate, as if *Alphonso,*
Still alive, were arming in *Valentia:*
Which wears indeed this Colour of a Truth,
They who are fled have that Way bent their Course.
Of the same Nature divers Notes have been
Dispers'd, t'amuze the People; whereupon
Some ready of Belief have rais'd this Rumour:

44

That being sav'd upon the Coast of *Africk,*
He there disclos'd himself to *Albucacim,*
And by a secret Compact made with him,
Open'd the way to this Invasion;
While he himself, returning to *Valentia*
In private, undertook to raise this Tumult.

Zara. Ha! hear'st thou that? Is *Osmyn* then *Alphonso!*
O Heav'n! a thousand things occur
To my Remembrance now, that make it plain.
O certain Death for him, as sure Despair
For me, if it be known—If not, what Hope
Have I? Yet 'twere the lowest Baseness, now
To yield him up—No, I will still conceal him,
And try the Force of yet more Obligations.

Gons. 'Tis not impossible. Yet, it may be
That some Impostor has usurp'd his Name.
Your beauteous Captive *Zara* can inform,
If such a one, so 'scaping, was receiv'd,
At any time, in *Albucacim's* Court.

King. Pardon, fair Excellence, this long Neglect:
An unforeseen, unwelcome Hour of Business,
Has thrust between us and our while of Love;
But wearing now apace with ebbing Sand,
Will quickly waste, and give again the Day.

Zara. You're too secure: The Danger is more imminent
Than your high Courage suffers you to see;
While *Osmyn* lives, you are not safe.

King. His Doom
Is pass'd; if you revoke it not, he dies.

Zara. 'Tis well. By what I heard upon your Entrance,
I find I can unfold what yet concerns
You more. One that did call himself *Alphonso*
Was cast upon my Coast, as is reported,
And oft had private Conference with the King;
To what Effect I knew not then: But that
Alphonso privately departed, just
About the time our Arms embark'd for *Spain.*
What I know more is, That a tripple League
Of strictest Friendship, was profess'd between
Alphonso, Heli, and the Traitor *Osmyn.*

King. Publick Report is ratify'd in this.

Zara. And *Osmyn's* Death requir'd of strong necessity.

King. Give Order strait that all the Pris'ners die,
We will our self behold the Execution.

Zara. Forbear a Moment; somewhat more I have
Worthy your private Ear, and this your Minister

King. Let all else 'void the Room. *Garcia,* give Order
For doubling all our Guards; command that our
Militia are in Arms: We will anon
Ride forth, and view the Order of our Troops.

[Exeunt *Garcia, Perez,* and *Attendants.*

Zara. I am your Captive, and you've us'd me nobly;
And in return of that, tho' otherwise
Your Enemy, I have discover'd *Osmyn*
His private Practice and Conspiracy
Against your State: And fully to discharge
My self of what I've undertaken, now
I think it fit to tell you, that your Guards
Are tainted; some among 'em have resolv'd
To rescue *Osmyn* at the Place of Death.

King. Is Treason then so near us as our Guards!

Zara. Most certain; tho' my Knowledge is not yet
So ripe, to point at the particular Men.

King. What's to be done?

Zara. That too I will advise.
I have remaining in my Train some Mutes,
A Present once from the *Sultana* Queen,
In the *Grand Signior*'s Court. These, from their Infancy,
Are practis'd in the Trade of Death; and shall
(As there the Custom is) in private strangle
Osmyn.

Gons. My Lord, the Queen advises well.

King. What Off'ring, or what Recompence remains
In me, that can be worthy of so great Services?
To cast beneath your Feet the Crown you've sav'd,
Though on the Head that wears it, were too little.

Zara. Of that hereafter; but, mean time, 'tis fit
You order none may have Admittance to
The Pris'ner, but such Messengers as I
Shall send.

King. Who waits there?

Enter *Perez.*

On your Life take heed,
That only *Zara*'s Mutes, or such who bring
Her Warrant, have Admittance to the *Moor.*

Zara. They and no other, not the Princess self.

46

Perez. Your Majesty shall be obey'd.

King. Retire.

Gons. That Interdiction so particular,
Pronounc'd with Vehemence against the Princess,
Should have more Meaning than appears bare-fac'd.
The King is blinded by his Love, and heeds
It not. Your Majesty sure might have spared
That last Restraint; you hardly can suspect
The Princess is Confederate with the *Moor.*

Zara. I've heard, her Charity did once extend
So far to visit him, at his Request.

Gons. Ha!

King. How? she visit *Osmyn!* What, my Daughter?

Selim. Madam, take heed; or you have ruin'd all.

Zara. And after did sollicite you on his
Behalf.—

King. Never. You have been mis-inform'd.

Zara. Indeed? Then 'twas a Whisper spread by some
Who wish'd it so; a common Art in Courts.
I will retire, and instantly prepare
Instruction for my Ministers of Death.

[Exeunt *Zara* and *Selim.*

Gons. There's somewhat yet of Mystery in this;
Her Words and Actions are obscure and double,
Sometimes concur, and sometimes disagree;
I like it not.

King. What dost thou think, *Gonsalez;*
Are we not much indebted to this Fair one?

Gons. I am a little slow of Credit, Sir,
In the Sincerity of Womens Actions.
Methinks this Lady's Hatred to the *Moor,*
Disquiets her too much; which makes it seem
As if she'd rather that she did not hate him.
I wish her Mutes are meant to be employ'd
As she pretends—I doubt it now—Your Guards
Corrupted; how? by whom? who told her so?
I'th' Evening *Osmyn* was to die; at Mid-night
She begg'd the Royal Signet to release him;
I'th' Morning he must die again; e'er Noon
Her Mutes alone must Strangle him or he'll
Escape. This put together suits not well.

King. Yet, that there's Truth in what she has discover'd,

47

Is manifest from every Circumstance.
This Tumult, and the Lords who fled with *Heli,*
Are Confirmation—that *Alphonso* lives,
Agrees expresly too with her Report.

Gons. I grant it, Sir; and doubt not, but in Rage
Of Jealousie, she has discover'd what
She now repents. It may be I'm deceiv'd.
But why that needless Caution of the Princess?
What if she had seen *Osmyn?* though 'twere strange.
But if she had, what was't to her? unless
She fear'd her stronger Charms might cause the *Moor's*
Affection to revolt.

King. I thank thee, Friend.
There's Reason in thy Doubt, and I am warn'd.
But think'st thou that my Daughter saw this *Moor?*

Gons. If *Osmyn* be, as *Zara* has related,
Alphonso's Friend; 'tis not impossible,
But she might wish on his Account to see him.

King. Say'st thou? by Heav'n thou hast arouz'd a Thought,
That like a sudden Earth-quake, shakes my Frame;
Confusion! then my Daughter's an Accomplice,
And plots in private with this hellish *Moor.*

Gons. That were too hard a Thought—but see she comes.
'Twere not amiss to question her a little,
And try howe'er, if I've divin'd aright.
If what I fear be true, she'll be concern'd
For *Osmyn's* Death, as he's *Alphonso's* Friend.
Urge that, to try if she'll sollicite for him.

Enter Almeria and Leonora.

King. Your coming has prevented me, *Almeria;*
I had determin'd to have sent for you.
Let your Attendant be dismiss'd; I have

[Exit Leonora.

To talk with you. Come near, why dost thou shake?
What mean those swollen and red-fleck'd Eyes, that look
As they had wept in Blood, and worn the Night
In waking Anguish? Why this, on the Day
Which was design'd to Celebrate thy Nuptials?
But that the Beams of Light are to be stain'd
With reeking Gore, from Traitors on the Rack:
Wherefore I have deferr'd the Marriage-Rites,
Nor shall the guilty Horrors of this Day
Prophane that Jubilee.

Alm. All Days to me

48

Henceforth are equal; this the Day of Death,
To morrow, and the next, and each that follows,
Will undistinguish'd roll, and but prolong
One hated Line of more extended Woe.

King. Whence is thy Grief? Give me to know the Cause,
And look thou answer me with Truth; for know,
I am not unacquainted with thy Falshood.
Why art thou mute? base and degenerate Maid!

Gons. Dear Madam, speak, or you'll incense the King.

Alm. What is't to speak? or wherefore should I speak?
What mean these Tears, but Grief unutterable?

King. Yes, Guilt; they are the dumb Confessions of
Thy guilty Mind; and say thou wert Confed'rate
With damn'd Conspirators to take my Life.
O impious Parricide! now canst thou speak?

Alm. O Earth, behold, I kneel upon thy Bosom,
And bend my flowing Eyes, to stream upon
Thy Face, imploring thee that thou wilt yield;
Open thy Bowels of Compassion, take
Into thy Womb the last and most forlorn
Of all thy Race. Hear me, thou common Parent;
—I have no Parent else—be thou a Mother,
And step between me and the Curse of him,
That was—that was, but is no more a Father.
But brands my Innocence with horrid Crimes,
And for the tender Names of Child and Daughter,
Now calls me Murderer and Parricide.

King. Rise, I command thee rise—and if thou wou'dst
Acquit thy self of those detested Names,
Swear thou hast never seen that Foreign Dog,
Now doom'd to die, that most accursed *Osmyn*.

Alm. Never, but as with Innocence I might,
And free of all bad Purposes. So Heav'n's
My Witness.

King. Vile equivocating Wretch!
With Innocence? Death and Perdition, she
Confesses it. By Heav'n I'll have him rack'd,
Torn, mangl'd, flay'd, impal'd—all Pains and Tortures
That Wit of Man and Dire Revenge can think,
Shall he accumulated under-bear.

Alm. Oh, I am lost—there Fate begins to wound.

King. Hear me, then, if thou canst reply, know, Traitress,
I'm not to learn that curs'd *Alphonso* lives;
Nor am I ignorant what *Osmyn* is.—

49

Alm. Then all is ended, and we both must die,
Since thou'rt reveal'd, alone thou shalt not die.
And yet alone would I have dy'd, Heav'n knows,
Repeated Deaths, rather than have reveal'd thee.
Yes, all my Father's wounding Wrath, tho' each
Reproach cuts deeper than the keenest Sword,
And cleaves my Heart; I would have born it all,
Nay, all the Pains that are prepar'd for thee:
To the remorseless Rack I would have given
This weak and tender Flesh, to have been bruis'd
And torn, rather than have reveal'd thy Being.

King. Hell, Hell! do I hear this, and yet endure!
What, dar'st thou to my Face avow thy Guilt?
Hence, e'er I curse—flie my just Rage, with speed;
Lest I forget us both, and spurn thee from me.

Alm. And yet a Father! think I am your Child.
Turn not your Eyes away—look on me kneeling;
Now curse me if you can, now spurn me off.
Did ever Father curse his kneeling Child!
Never: For always Blessings crown that Posture.
Nature inclines, and half-way meets that Duty,
Stooping to raise from Earth the Filial Reverence;
For bended Knees returning folding Arms,
With Pray'rs, and Blessings, and paternal Love.
O hear me then, thus crawling on the Earth—

King. Be thou advis'd, and let me go, while yet
The light Impression thou hast made remains.

Alm. No, never will I rise, nor loose this Hold,
'Till you are mov'd, and grant that he may live.

King. Ha! who may live? take heed, no more of that;
For on my Soul he dies, tho' thou, and I,
And all should follow to partake his Doom.
Away, off, let me go.—Call her Attendants.

                    Enter *Leonora* and Attendants.

Alm. Drag me, harrow the Earth with my bare Bosom,
I'll not let go 'till you have spar'd my Husband.

King. Ha! what say'st thou? Husband! Husband! Damnation!
What Husband? which? who?

Alm. He, he is my Husband.

King. Poison and Daggers! who?

Alm. O—

[*Faints*

Gons. Help, support her.

Alm. Let me go, let me fall, sink deep—I'll dig,
I'll dig a Grave, and tear up Death; I will;
I'll scrape 'till I collect his rotten Bones,
And cloath their Nakedness with my own Flesh;
Yes, I will strip of Life, and we will change:
I will be Death; then tho' you kill my Husband
He shall be mine, still and for ever mine.

King. What Husband? who? whom dost thou mean?

Gons. Alas, she raves!

Alm. O that I did. *Osmyn,* he is my Husband.

King. Osmyn!

Alm. Not *Osmyn,* but *Alphonso* is my dear
And wedded Husband—Heav'n, and Air, and Seas,
Ye Winds and Waves, I call ye all to witness.

King. Wilder than Winds or Waves thy self dost rave.
Should I hear more, I too should catch thy Madness.
Yet somewhat she must mean of dire Import,
Which I'll not hear, 'till I am more at Peace.
Watch her returning Sense, and bring me Word:
And look that she attempt not on her Life.

[Ex. King.

Alm. O stay, yet stay; hear me, I am not mad.
I would to Heav'n I were—He's gone!

Gons. Have Comfort.

Alm. Curs'd be that Tongue, that bids me be of Comfort;
Curs'd my own Tongue, that cou'd not move his Pity;
Curs'd these weak Hands, that cou'd not hold him here;
For he is gone to doom *Alphonso*'s Death.

Gons. Your too excessive Grief works on your Fancy,
And deludes your Sense. *Alphonso,* if living,
Is far from hence, beyond your Father's Power.

Alm. Hence, thou detested, ill-tim'd Flatterer;
Source of my Woes: Thou and thy Race be curs'd;
But doubly thou, who could'st alone have Policy
And Fraud, to find the fatal Secret out,
And know that *Osmyn* was *Alphonso.*

Gons. Ha!

Alm. Why dost thou start? What dost thou see or hear?
Was it the doleful Bell, tolling for Death?
Or dying Groans from my *Alphonso*'s Breast?
See, see, look yonder! where a grizzled, pale,
And ghastly Head glares by, all smear'd with Blood,
Gasping as it would speak; and after it,

51

Behold a damp, dead Hand has dropp'd a Dagger:
I'll catch it—Hark! a Voice cries Murder! 'tis
My Father's Voice; hollow it sounds, and from
The Tomb it calls—I'll follow it; for there
I shall again behold my dear *Alphonso*.

[Exit with *Attendants*.

Gons. She's greatly griev'd; nor am I less surpriz'd.
Osmyn Alphonso! no; she over-rates
My Policy! I ne'er suspected it:
Nor now had known it, but from her Mistake.
Her Husband too! Ha! Where is *Garcia* then?
And where the Crown that should descend on him,
To grace the Line of my Posterity?
Hold, let me think—if I should tell the King—
Things come to this Extremity? his Daughter
Wedded already—what if he should yield?
Knowing no Remedy for what is past;
And urg'd by Nature pleading for his Child,
With which he seems to be already shaken.
And tho' I know he hates beyond the Grave
Anselmo's Race; yet if—that If concludes me.
To doubt, when I may be assur'd, is Folly.
But how prevent the Captive Queen, who means
To set him free? Ay, now 'tis plain; O well
Invented Tale! He was *Alphonso's* Friend.
This subtle Woman will amuze the King,
If I delay—'twill do—or better so.
One to my Wish. *Alonzo,* thou art welcome.

Enter *Alonzo*.

Alon. The King expects your Lordship.

Gons. 'Tis no matter.
I'm not i'th' way at present, good *Alonzo.*

Alon. If't please your Lordship, I'll return, and say
I have not seen you.

Gons. Do, my best *Alonzo.*
Yet stay, I would—but go; anon will serve—
Yet I have that requires thy speedy help.
I think thou would'st not stop to do me Service.

Alon. I am your Creature.

Gons. Say thou art my Friend.
I've seen thy Sword do Noble Execution.

Alon. All that it can your Lordship shall command.

Gons. Thanks; and I take thee at thy Word. Thou'st seen,
Among the Followers of the Captive Queen,

Dumb Men, that make their Meaning known by Signs.

Alon. I have, my Lord.

Gons. Could'st thou procure, with Speed
And Privacy, the wearing Garb of one
Of those, tho' purchas'd by his Death, I'd give
Thee such Reward, as should exceed thy Wish.

Alon. Conclude it done. Where shall I wait your Lordship?

Gons. At my Appartment. Use thy utmost Diligence;
Away, I've not been seen—haste, good *Alonzo.*

[Ex. *Alon.*

So, this can hardly fail. *Alphonso* slain,
The greatest Obstacle is then remov'd.
Almeria widow'd, yet again may wed;
And I yet fix the Crown on *Garcia*'s Head.

[Exit.

Act V.
Scene I.
A Room of State.
Enter *King, Perez* and *Alonzo.*

King. NOT to be found? In an ill Hour he's absent.
None, say you, none? what not the Fav'rite Eunuch?
Nor she her self, nor any of her Mutes,
Have yet requir'd Admittance?

Perez. None, my Lord.

King. Is *Osmyn* so dispos'd as I commanded?

Perez. Fast bound in double Chains, and at full length
He lyes supine on Earth; as easily
She might remove the fix'd Foundation, as
Unlock the Rivets of his Bonds.

King. 'Tis well.

[A Mute appears, and seeing the *King* retires.

Ha! seize that Mute; *Alonzo,* follow him.

[Ex. *Alonzo.*

Ent'ring he met my Eyes, and started back,
Frighted, and fumbling one Hand in his Bosom,
As to conceal th' Importance of his Errand.

[*Alonzo* re-enters with a Paper.

Alon. O bloody Proof of obstinate Fidelity!

King. What dost thou mean?

Alon. Soon as I seiz'd the Man,
He snatch'd from out his Bosom this—and strove
With rash and greedy haste, at once to cram
The Morsel down his Throat. I catch'd his Arm,
And hardly wrench'd his Hand to wring it from him;
Which done, he drew a Ponyard from his Side,
And on the instant plung'd it in his Breast.

King. Remove the Body thence e'er *Zara* see it.

Alon. I'll be so bold to borrow his Attire;
'Twill quit me of my Promise to *Gonsalez.*

[Exit.

Perez. Whate'er it is the King's Complection turns.

King. How's this? my Mortal Foe beneath my Roof!

[*Having read the Letter.*

O, give me Patience, all ye Powers! no, rather
Give me Rage, Rage, implacable Revenge,

And trebled Fury—Ha! who's there?

Perez. My Lord.

King. Hence, Slave, how dar'st thou 'bide to watch and pry
Into how poor and mean a thing a King descends;
How like thy self, when Passion treads him down?
Ha! stir not, on thy Life: For thou wert fix'd,
And planted here to see me gorge this Bait,
And lash against the Hook—By Heav'n you're all
Rank Traitors; thou art with the rest combin'd;
Thou knew'st that *Osmyn* was *Alphonso,* knew'st
My Daughter privately conferr'd with him,
And wert the Spy and Pander to their Meeting.

Perez. By all that's Holy, I'm amaz'd.—

King. Thou ly'st.
Thou art Accomplice too much with *Zara;* here
Where she sets down—*Still will I set thee free—*

[*Reading.*

That somewhere is repeated—*I have Power
O'er them that are thy Guards*—Mark that, thou Traitor.

Perez. It was your Majesty's Command, I should
Obey her Order.—

King.

    Reading.

    *—And still will I set
Thee free,* Alphonso—Hell! curs'd, curs'd *Alphonso!*
False, perfidious *Zara!* Strumpet Daughter!
Away, be gone, thou feeble Boy, fond Love,
All Nature, Softness, Pity and Compassion,
This Hour I throw thee off, and entertain
Fell Hate, within my Breast, Revenge and Gall.
By Heav'n I'll meet, and counterwork this Treachery.
Hark thee, Villain, Traitor—answer me, Slave.

Perez. My Service has not merited those Titles.

King. Dar'st thou reply? Take that—thy Service? thine?

[*Strikes him.*

What's thy whole Life, thy Soul, thy All, to my
One Moment's Ease? Hear my Command; and look
That thou obey, or Horror on thy Head.
Drench me thy Dagger in *Alphonso's* Heart.
Why dost thou start? Resolve to do't, or else—

Perez. My Lord, I will.

King. 'Tis well—that when she comes to set him free,

56

His Teeth may grin, and mock at her Remorse.

[*Perez* going.

—Stay thee—I've farther thought—I'll add to this,
And give her Eyes yet greater Disappointment.
When thou hast ended him, bring me his Robe;
And let the Cell where she'll expect to see him
Be darken'd, so as to amuse the Sight.
I'll be conducted thither—
But see she comes; I'll shun th' Encounter; do
Thou follow, and give heed to my Direction.

[Exeunt.

Enter *Zara* and *Selim*.

Zara. The Mute not yet return'd! 'tis strange. Ha! 'twas
The King that parted hence; frowning he went;
His Eyes like Meteors roll'd, then darted down
Their red and angry Beams; as if his Sight
Would, like the raging Dog-star, scorch the Earth,
And kindle Ruin in its Course. Think'st thou
He saw me not?

Selim. He did: But then as if.
His Eyes had err'd, he hastily recall'd
Th' imperfect Look, and sternly turn'd away.

Zara. Shun me when seen! I fear thou hast undone me.
Thy shallow Artifice begets Suspicion,
And, like a Cobweb-Veil, but thinly shades
The Face of thy Design; alone disguising
What should have ne'er been seen; imperfect Mischief!
Thou like the Adder, venomous and deaf,
Hast stung the Traveller; and, after, hear'st
Not his pursuing Voice; ev'n where thou think'st
To hide, the rustling Leaves and bended Grass
Consess, and point the Path which thou hast crept.
O Fate of Fools! officious in Contriving;
In Executing puzzled, lame and lost.

Selim. Avert it, Heav'n, that thou should ever suffer
For my Defect; or that the Means which I
Devis'd to serve should ruin your Design!
Prescience is Heav'n's alone, not giv'n to Man.
If I have fail'd in what, as being a Man,
I needs must fail; impute not as a Crime
My Nature's want, but punish Nature in me:
I plead not for a Pardon and to live,
But to be punish'd and forgiven. Here, strike;
I bare my Breast to meet your just Revenge.

57

Zara. I have not leisure now to take so poor
A Forfeit as thy Life: Somewhat of high
And more important Fate requires my Thought.
When I've concluded on my self, if I
Think fit, I'll leave thee my Command to die.
Regard me well; and dare not to reply
To what I give in Charge; for I'm resolv'd.
Instruct the two remaining Mutes, that they
Attend me instantly, with each a Bowl
Of those Ingredients mix'd, as will with speed
Benumn the living Faculties, and give
Most easie and inevitable Death.
Yes, *Osmyn,* yes; be *Osmyn* or *Alphonso,*
I'll give thee Freedom, if thou dar'st be free:
Such Liberty as I embrace my self,
Thou shalt partake. Since Fates no more afford;
I can but die with thee to keep my Word.

[Exeunt.

Scene II.

Scene changes to the Prison.

Enter *Gonsalez,* disguis'd like a Mute, with a Dagger.

Gons. Nor Centinel, nor Guard! the Doors unbarr'd!
And all as still, as at the Noon of Night!
Sure Death already has been busie here.
There lies my Way, that Door is too unlock'd.

[*Looks in.*

Ha! sure he sleeps—all's dark within, save what
A Lamp, that feebly lifts a sickly Flame,
By fits reveals—his Face seems turn'd to favour
Th' Attempt: I'll steal, and do it unperceiv'd.
What Noise! some body coming? 'st, *Alonzo?*
No body? Sure he'll wait without—I would
'Twere done—I'll crawl, and sting him to the Heart;
Then cast my Skin, and leave it there to answer it.

[*Goes in.*

Enter *Garcia* and *Alonzo.*

Gar. Where? where, *Alonzo?* where's my Father? where
The King? Confusion! all is on the Rout!
All's lost, all ruin'd by Surprize and Treachery.
Where, where is he? Why dost thou thus miss-lead me?

Alon. My Lord, he enter'd but a moment since,
And could not pass me unperceiv'd—What hoa!
My Lord, my Lord, what, hoa! My Lord *Gonsalez!*

Enter *Gonsalez* bloody.

Gons. Perdition choak your Clamours—whence this Rudeness?
Garcia!

Gar. Perdition, Slavery, and Death,
Are entring now our Doors. Where is the King?
What means this Blood? and why this Face of Horror?

Gons. No matter—give me first to know the Cause
Of these your rash and ill-tim'd Exclamations.

Gar. The Eastern Gate is to the Foe betray'd,
Who but for Heaps of Slain, that choak the Passage,
Had enter'd long e'er now, and born down all
Before 'em, to the Palace Walls. Unless
The King in Person animate our Men
Granada's lost; and to confirm this Fear,
The Traitor *Perez,* and the Captive *Moor,*
Are through a Postern fled, and join the Foe.

Gons. Would all were false as that; for whom you call
The *Moor* is dead. That *Osmyn* was *Alphonso;*
In whose Heart's Blood this Ponyard yet is warm.

Gar. Impossible; for *Osmyn* flying, was
Pronounc'd aloud by *Perez* for *Alphonso.*

Gons. Enter that Chamber, and convince your Eyes,
How much Report has wrong'd your easie Faith.

[*Garcia* goes in.

Alon. My Lord, for certain Truth *Perez* is fled;
And has declar'd the Cause of his Revolt,
Was to revenge a Blow the King had giv'n him.

Gar. (returning.) Ruin and Horror! O heart-wounding Sight!

Gons. What says my Son? what Ruin? ha? what Horror?

Gar. Blasted my Eyes, and speechless be my Tongue,
Rather than or to see, or to relate
This Deed—O dire Mistake! O fatal Blow!
The King—

Gons. Alon. The King!

Gar. Dead, welt'ring, drown'd in Blood.
See, see, attir'd like *Osmyn,* where he lies.

[*They go in.*

O whence, or how, or wherefore was this done?
But what imports the Manner, or the Cause?
Nothing remains to do, or to require,
But that we all should turn our Swords against
Our selves, and expiate with our own his Blood.

59

Gons. O Wretch! O curs'd, and rash, deluded Fool!
On me, on me, turn your avenging Sword.
I, who have spilt my Royal Master's Blood,
Should make Atonement by a Death as horrid;
And fall beneath the Hand of my own Son.

Gar. Ha! what? atone this Murder with a greater!
The Horror of that Thought has damp'd my Rage.
The Earth already groans to bear this Deed;
Oppress her not, nor think to stain her Face
With more unnatural Blood. Murder my Father!
Better with this to rip up my own Bowels,
And bathe it to the Hilt, in far less damnable
Self-Murder.

Gons. O my Son, from the blind Dotage
Of a Father's Fondness these Ills arose;
For thee I've been ambitious, base, and bloody:
For thee I've plung'd into this Sea of Sin;
Stemming the Tide with one weak Hand, and bearing
With the other the Crown, to wreath thy Brow,
Whose Weight has sunk me e'er I reach'd the Shoar.

Gar. Fatal Ambition! Hark! the Foe is enter'd:

[*Shout.*

The Shrilness of that Shout speaks 'em at hand.
We have no time to search into the Cause
Of this surprizing and most fatal Error.
What's to be done? The King's Death known, will strike
The few remaining Soldiers with Despair,
And make 'em yield to Mercy of the Conqueror.

Alon. My Lord, I've thought how to conceal the Body;
Require me not to tell the Means, 'till done,
Lest you forbid what then you may approve.

[*Goes in.*

[*Shout.*

Gons. They shout again! Whate'er he means to do,
'Twere fit the Soldiers were amus'd mean time
With Hopes, and fed with Expectation of
The King's immediate Presence at their Head.

Gar. Were it a Truth, I fear 'tis now too late.
But I'll omit no Care, nor Haste; and try
Or to repel their Force, or bravely die.

[Exit.

Gons. What hast thou done, *Alonzo?*

Alon. Such a Deed

60

As but an Hour ago I'd not have done,
Tho' for the Crown of Universal Empire.
But what are Kings reduc'd to common Clay?
Or who can wound the Dead?—I've from the Body
Sever'd the Head, and in a Corner of
The Room dispos'd it, muffled in the Mute's
Attire; leaving alone to View, the bloody
And undistinguishable Trunk:
Which may be still mistaken by the Guards
For *Osmyn,* if in seeking for the King
They chance to find it.

Gons. 'Twas an Act of Horror;
And of a piece with this Day's dire Misdeeds.
But 'tis not yet the time to ponder, or
Repent. Haste thee, *Alonzo,* hence, with speed,
To aid my Son. I'll follow with the last
Reserve, to re-inforce his Arms: At least,
I shall make good, and shelter his Retreat.

                                              [Exeunt.

      Enter *Zara,* follow'd by *Selim,* and two Mutes bearing the Bowls.

Zara. Silence and Solitude are ev'ry where!
Thro' all the Gloomy Ways and Iron Doors
That hither lead, nor Human Face nor Voice
Is seen or heard. A dreadful Din was wont
To grate the Sense, when enter'd here; from Groans
And Howls of Slaves condemn'd, from Clink of Chains,
And Crash of rusty Bars and creeking Hinges:
And ever and anon the Sight was dash'd
With frightful Faces, and the meagre Looks
Of grim and gastly Executioners.
Yet more this Stilness terrifies my Soul,
Than did that Scene of complicated Horrors.
It may be, that the Cause and Purpose of
My Errand, being chang'd from Life to Death,
Has also wrought this chilling Change of Temper.
Or does my Heart bode more? what can it more
Than Death?—
Let 'em set down the Bowls, and warn *Alphonso*
That I am here—so. You return and find

[*Mutes going in.*

The King; tell him, what he requir'd, I've done,
And wait his coming to approve the Deed.

                                              [Exit *Selim.*

What have you seen? Ha! wherefore stare you thus,

[The *Mutes* return, and look affrighted.

With haggar'd Eyes? why are your Arms a-cross?
Your heavy and desponding Heads hung down?
Why is't you more than speak in these sad Signs?
Give me more ample Knowledge of this Mourning.

They go to the Scene, which opens and shews the Body.

Ha! prostrate! bloody! headless! O—start Eyes,
Split Heart, burst ev'ry Vein, at this dire Object:
At once dissolve and flow; meet Blood with Blood;
Dash your encount'ring Streams with mutual Violence,
'Till Surges roll and foaming Billows rise,
And curl their Crimson Heads to kiss the Clouds!
—Rain, rain ye Stars, spout from your burning Orbs
Precipitated Fires, and pour in Sheets
The blazing Torrent on the Tyrant's Head;
Scorch and consume the curs'd perfidious King.

Enter Selim.

Selim. I've sought in vain, the King is no where to
Be found—

Zara. Get thee to Hell, and seek him there.

[*Stabs him.*

His Hellish Rage had wanted Means to act,
But for thy fatal and pernicious Counsel.

Selim. You thought it better then—but I'm rewarded.
The Mute you sent, by some Mischance was seen,
And forc'd to yield your Letter with his Life:
I found the dead and bloody Body stripp'd—
My Tongue faulters, and my Voice fails—
Drink not the Poison—for *Alphonso* is—

[*Dies.*

Zara. As thou art now—And I shall quickly be.
'Tis not that he is dead; for 'twas decreed
We both should die. Nor is't that I survive;
I have a Remedy for that. But Oh,
He dy'd unknowing in my Heart.
He knew I lov'd, but knew not to what height:
Nor that I meant to fall before his Eyes,
A Martyr and a Victim to my Vows:
Insensible of this last Proof he's gone.
Yet Fate alone can rob his Mortal Part
Of Sense: His Soul still sees, and knows each Purpose,
And fix'd Event of my persisting Faith.
Then, wherefore do I pause?—give me the Bowl.

[*A* Mute *kneels and gives one of the Bowls.*

Hover a Moment, yet, thou gentle Spirit,

Soul of my Love, and I will wait thy Flight.
This to our mutual Bliss when join'd above.

[*Drinks.*

O friendly Draught, already in my Heart!
Cold, cold; my Veins are Icicles and Frost.
I'll creep into his Bosom, lay me there;
Cover us close—or I shall chill his Breast,
And fright him from my Arms—See, see, he slides
Still further from me; look, he hides his Face,
I cannot feel it—quite beyond my reach.
O now he's gone, and all is dark—

[*Dies.*

[The *Mutes* kneel and mourn over her.

Enter *Almeria* and *Leonora.*

Alm. O let me seek him in this horrid Cell;
For in the Tomb or Prison, I alone
Must hope to find him.

Leo. Heav'ns! what dismal Scene
Of Death is this? The Eunuch *Selim* slain!

Alm. Shew me, for I am come in search of Death;
But want a Guide; for Tears have dimn'd my Sight.

Leo. Alas, a little farther, and behold
Zara all pale and dead! two frightful Men,
Who seem the Murderers, kneel weeping by:
Feeling Remorse too late for what they've done.
But O forbear—lift up your Eyes no more;
But haste away, fly from this Fatal Place,
Where Miseries are multiply'd; return
And look not on; for there's a Dagger that
Will stab the Sight, and make your Eyes rain Blood.

Alm. O I foresee that Object in my Mind.
Is it at last then so? is he then dead?
What dead at last, quite, quite, for ever dead?
There, there I see him; there he lies, the Blood
Yet bubbling from his Wounds—O more than Savage!
Had they, or Hearts, or Eyes, that did this Deed?
Could Eyes endure to guide such cruel Hands?
Are not my Eyes guilty alike with theirs,
That thus can gaze, and yet not turn to Stone?
—I do not weep! The Springs of Tears are dry'd;
And of a sudden I am calm, as if
All things were well; and yet my Husband's murder'd!
Yes, yes, I know to mourn; I'll Sluce this Heart,
The Source of Woe, and let the Torrent loose.

—Those Men have left to weep, and look on me;
I hope they murder all on whom they look.
Behold me well; your bloody Hands have err'd,
And wrongfully have put to Death those Innocents:
I am the Sacrifice design'd to bleed;
And come prepar'd to yield my Throat—they shake
Their Heads in sign of Grief and Innocence!

[*They point at the Bowl on the Ground.*

And point! what mean they? Ha! a Cup. O well
I understand what Medicine has been here.
O noble Thirst! and yet too greedy to
Drink all—O for another Draught of Death.

[*They point at the other Cup.*

Ha! point again? 'tis there, and full, I hope.
O thanks the liberal Hand that fill'd thee thus;
I'll drink my glad Acknowledgment—

Leo. O hold
For Mercy's sake; upon my Knees—forbear.—

Alm. With Thee the kneeling World should beg in vain,
Seest thou not there who prostrate lyes,
And pleads against thee? who shall then prevail?
Yet I will take a cold and parting Leave,
From his pale Lips; I'll kiss him e'er I drink,
Lest the rank Juice should blister on my Mouth,
And stain the Colour of my last Adieu.
Horror! a headless Trunk! nor Lips nor Face,

[*Coming nearer the Body, starts and lets fall the Cup.*

But spouting Veins, and mangled Flesh! O, O.

    Enter *Alphonso, Heli, Perez,* with *Garcia* Prisoner, Guards and Attendants.

Alph. Away, stand off, where is she? let me fly,
Save her from Death; and snatch her to my Heart.

Alm. Oh—

Alph. Forbear; my Arms alone shall hold her up:
Warm her to Life, and wake her into Gladness.
O let me talk to thy reviving Sense,
The Words of Joy and Peace; warm thy cold Beauties,
With the new-flushing Ardour of my Cheek;
Into thy Lips, pour the soft trickling Balm
Of Cordial Sighs; and reinspire thy Bosom
With the Breath of Love. Shine, awake, *Almeria,*
Give a new Birth to thy long-shaded Eyes,
Then double on the Day reflected Light.

Alm. Where am I? Heav'n! what does this Dream intend?

Alph. O may'st thou never dream of less Delight,
Nor ever wake to less substantial Joys.

Alm. Giv'n me again from Death! O all ye Pow'rs
Confirm this Miracle! can I believe
My Sight, against my Sight? and shall I trust
That Sense, which in one Instant shews him dead
And living? Yes, I will; I've been abus'd
With Apparitions and affrighting Fantoms:
This is my Lord, my Life, my only Husband;
I have him now, and we no more will part.
My Father too shall have Compassion—

Alph. O my Heart's Comfort; 'tis not giv'n to this
Frail Life, to be entirely bless'd. Even now,
In this extreamest Joy my Soul can taste,
Yet am I dash'd to think that thou must weep;
Thy Father fell, where he design'd my Death.
Gonsalez and *Alonzo,* both of Wounds
Expiring, have with their last Breath confess'd
The just Decrees of Heav'n, in turning on
Themselves their own most bloody Purposes.
Nay, I must grant, 'tis fit you shou'd be thus—

[*She weeps.*

Let 'em remove the Body from her Sight.
Ill-fated *Zara!* Ha! a Cup? alas!
Thy Error then is plain; but I were Flint
Not to o'er-flow in Tribute to thy Memory.
She shall be Royally Interr'd. O *Garcia,*
Whose Virtue has renounc'd thy Father's Crimes,
Seest thou, how just the Hand of Heav'n has been?
Let us that thro' our Innocence survive,
Still in the Paths of Honour persevere,
And not from past or present Ills despair:
For Blessings ever wait on virtuous Deeds;
And tho' a late, a sure Reward succeeds.

[Exeunt Omnes.

Epilogue

Spoken by Mrs. *Bracegirdle*.

THE Tragedy thus done, I am, you know,
No more a Princess, but *in statu quo*:
And now as unconcern'd this Mourning wear,
As if indeed a Widow, or an Heir.
I've leisure, now, to mark your sev'ral Faces,
And know each Critick by his sour Grimaces.
To poison Plays, I see some where they sit,
Scatter'd, like Rats-bane, up and down the Pit;
While others watch like Parish-Searchers, hir'd
To tell of what Disease the Play expir'd.
O with what Joy they run, to spread the News
Of a damn'd Poet, and departed Muse!
But if he 'scape, with what Regret they're seiz'd!
And how they're disappointed if they're pleas'd!
Criticks to Plays for the same end resort,
That Surgeons wait on Trials in a Court;
For Innocence condemn'd they've no Respect,
Provided they've a Body to dissect.
As *Sussex* Men, that dwell upon the Shoar,
Look out when Storms arise, and Billows roar,
Devoutly praying, with uplifted Hands,
That some well-laden Ship may strike the Sands;
To whose Rich Cargo they may make Pretence,
And fatten on the Spoils of Providence:
So Criticks throng to see a New Play split,
And thrive and prosper on the Wrecks of Wit.
Small Hope our Poet from these Prospects draws;
And therefore to the Fair commends his Cause
Your tender Hearts to Mercy are inclin'd,
With whom, he hopes, this Play will Favour find,
Which was an Off'ring to the Sex design'd.

Printed in Great Britain
by Amazon

18584793R00047